Faster

After Baby

Field notes from the crossroads of competitive running & pregnancy

By Meredith Mikell

Copyright © 2015 by Meredith Mikell

Cover design and photography by E. Stephen Mikell Sr. and Meredith Mikell

All rights reserved. No part of this book may be reproduced, scanned, or distributed in any printed or electronic form without express permission from the author or publisher.

This book is in no way a substitute for medical expertise. The author does not intend to provide advice contrary to that of a physician.

First Edition: August 2015

ISBN-10: 1517086264

ISBN-13: 978-1517086268

Printed in the United States of America

For more information or permissions, contact Meredith Mikell:

www.runnervation.com

To my sons, Stephen Jr and Jack. You bring me so much joy, laughter, and hope, every day.

Contents

Contents 4
List of Figures 6
About This Book 9
Preface 11
PART I – YOU RUNNING 15
Chapter 1 – Why Do We Run? 17
Chapter 2 – Why Don't We Run? 23
Chapter 3 - Building Your Team 33
Chapter 4 - Setting Goals 39
PART II – YOU EXPECTING 47
Chapter 5 – Your Pregnant Running Body: The Basics 49
Chapter 6 – Your Pregnant Running Body: Beyond the Basics 63
Chapter 7 – Nutrition & Pregnancy 79
Chapter 8 – Keeping Perspective 87
PART III – YOU RECOVERING 97
Chapter 9– Postpartum Running: The Basics 99
Chapter 10 – Postpartum Running: Beyond the Basics 109
Chapter 11 – The Nursing Runner 121
Chapter 12 – Life As You Know It 131
PART IV – YOU SUCCEEDING 147
Chapter 13 – Getting Faster 149
Chapter 14 – Staying Healthy 161
Chapter 15 – Get Strong 177
Chapter 16 – The Long Road Ahead 191
Acknowledgements 197
Favorite Resources 199

Great Blogs & Sites 199
References 201
    Image Credits 206
About the Author 209

List of Figures

Figure 1- The Round Ligament 53
Figure 2 – Center of gravity and spinal changes, both before and during pregnancy 56
Figure 3- The Borg Rating of Perceived Exertion (RPE) 59
Figure 4- The spreading of the pelvis during pregnancy 66
Figure 5- A bridge analogy for the strain pelvic tilting places on hip & gluteal muscles 67
Figure 6 - These muscles are at the crux of your running ability. 68
Figure 7 - How the change in hip spreading affects your legs, ankles, and feet. 72
Figure 8 – Spreading of abdominal muscles. 74
Figure 9 - Upright push-ups: improve your overall core strength and posture without putting too much strain on your abdominals. Like regular push-ups, only vertical. 76
Figure 10 - Squats against the wall. You want your back to be straight and focus on "being tall", without feeling too much strain in your mid to lower abdominals (underneath hand). This is great for strengthening your hamstrings and hips, too. 76
Figure 11 - Seated squeeze & core contraction. Place your hand on your mid-abdominals. Start with your back upright against the back of the chair (left). Inhale. When you exhale, gently contract your abdominals beneath your hand (right). Think of pressing your belly button to your spine. 77
Figure 12 - Laying head lift. Place your hand on your abdominals. Keep your back flat on the mat and your head relaxed (left). Gently lift your head from the mat, without doing a full crunch (right). You want to feel a slight squeeze in your abdominals but not fully engage them. If you have diastasis recti, you should feel a gap in your abdominals just between your fingers (where my hand is placed). 77
Figure 13 - Good form, running with one hand (left) and with both hands (right) on the hand bar. Back straight, foot landing directly under hips, elbows slightly bent. 108
Figure 14 – Baby thrust: like kettle bells, but with smiles! Keep your back straight and lift from the legs, engaging your hamstrings. 187

Figure 15 – Baby thrust: generally the same exercise as in Figure 17, but with baby facing forward. This may allow a little more "swing" during the squat phase, and likely result in more giggles. 188
Figure 16 – Baby lunge: can also be done by switching baby side to side, if he/she enjoys it. Keep your back straight and push off from the heels. .188
Figure 17 – Baby sit-up: there are many ways of doing this one. Best achieved with kiss at the top. 188

About This Book

It is my primary goal to equip you to enter into the joys of parenthood while continuing athletic success.

My book will take you through some of the lesser-known science on the intersection of pregnancy, breastfeeding, new parenthood, and competitive running.

I do go over "the basics" of these topics and also cover the lesser-known or emerging science, along with my own stories, injury prevention tips, and occasional running humor that you speedy sisters will likely appreciate.

We will explore the physical adaptations your body undergoes to build and support a baby while proceeding with training.

We will identify the many ways that running-related problems can strike, both the obvious and the less obvious culprits, during and after pregnancy.

You'll get a crash course in several aspects of running physiology, injury prevention, and nutrition.

You'll get recommendations for strength training, cross training, and optimizing your potential as a runner, both now and for years to come.

My story as a mother-runner is [hopefully] a helpful one to you, but it is just one out of a vast and diverse mosaic of others. We will, therefore, also explore the personal experiences of some of our training compatriots: veteran running mamas from across the spectrum of ability and goals, who are also passionate about the sport and want to share their journeys. Their reflections are quoted in my text but are also found throughout the book as segments titled *"Mighty Mamas."*

This book is not about losing baby weight after pregnancy or training for your first 5K.

It is not any kind of training plan though it will provide some suggestions on how to best approach training programs postpartum.

Finally, most importantly, this book is meant to provide hope and perspective on your present and future as a mother-runner!

Preface

I just came back from a run. A really special run. I set a personal best in the marathon, finished third overall female, and re-qualified for Boston. My son is 18 months old and this was my first full marathon since he was born. My victory was longer coming than I had originally wanted, as injury after injury plagued my training following his birth. During that time, I struggled to understand why I couldn't stay healthy, feared that I would never run fast again, and generally grappled with the role that running would take on in my life. My new, awkward relationship with running felt like I was reuniting with my best childhood friend, after we had grown up and changed, anxious that our cherished dynamic would never be the same. I am very confident that you, reader, have experienced precisely this. If not, then perhaps you will soon, in lieu of pregnancy or a major life change of another kind.

Like most of you, I am not an elite runner. Though certainly would love to be, one day. It's not too late. My running history started jogging the annual Bloomsday race in Spokane with my family when I was a small child, gained momentum in high school track and cross country, and took flight in my mid-twenties when I discovered that the marathon is what really makes me tick. Along the way I have been blessed with mentors, both coaches and colleagues, who have influenced my successes in immeasurable ways. But unlike collegiate and professional runners, I was not ever burdened with the pressure to win, at least not from anyone but myself. This is true of all of us "recreational runners", and therein are both upsides and downsides to this fact.

On one hand, our running life is purely and entirely our own creation, with nobody else's expectations or ambitions to confound it.

On the other hand - unless you *did* run in college - we missed out on the exceptional resources and high-octane competition during our youth, the immersion that can shift your athletic paradigm to a higher level than we can imagine for ourselves in local road races. This facet of competitive running may not be necessary to most non-professional runners, but for those of us ingrained with an insatiable desire to race at championships, attempt to win them, and push our otherwise ordinary selves into the throws of elitedom, it is a mental paradigm that we must cultivate on our own.

Most recreational runners are not as worried about hitting competitive race times, or achieving a certain age-grade, or qualifying for Boston. Most are in it for the very best reasons to run: the physical, emotional, and mental improvements running brings them. The prevailing running and training books on the market reflect this majority, with a much smaller assortment of academic literature focused on elite performances and maximizing the human athletic potential.

But there is a growing contingent of us who want more out of competitive running than the fitness gains, yet we are not professional runners. We are the "sub-elites". We can tell you what our VDOT is and how much time we spent at our lactic acid threshold on yesterday's run. We frequently win road races at the local level, and can tell you the names and PRs of the other fastest women in town. We set our sights on a Boston qualifying race, and when we hit our BQ, we start dreaming of the Olympic Trials. Our families and friends know exactly where to meet us for dinner during marathon taper week. We fit into a different running niche than both the average recreational runners and the elites. We train as hard as our non-running commitments allow, striking perhaps the maximum balance of training, personal lives, and professional lives, given that we are not professional athletes.

And many of us are mothers, which brings me to the most important reason why I wrote this book.

Pregnancy can obviously modify an athlete's career. It changes not only the way our bodies look and function, but also how we will be using them for some time to come. But the paradigm of women needing exclusive rest and the notion that athletic endeavors are hazardous to the health of mother and baby is nearly gone, save for some disapproving glances from well-intentioned members of an older generation when you run by. Instead, the social media sphere hints of an 'uber-parenting' paradigm that might have you believing any activity a parent dedicates themselves to outside of their baby to be a selfish endeavor. So do we have to choose between competitive running and motherhood? Can running while pregnant cause any harm to the baby?

Naturally, we look to the pros for examples of striking this balance. When pregnant, I read up on how famous elite marathoners trained, recovered and raced during pregnancy and in the following months. Paula Radcliffe and Kara Goucher had recently set personal bests and Olympic qualifying race times within a year of their pregnancies. And it wasn't just elites. Blogs and running magazine articles abounded with stories of women of all abilities running right up until they went into labor and delivering perfectly healthy babies. It appeared that as long as women were not in a high-risk pregnancy and didn't exert themselves *more than they did pre-pregnancy*, running was a 'go'.

I was going to nail this. As per my aforementioned competitive programming, my new training goal was to win at making a baby while continuing my training. Not "win" in the sense of out-performing anyone else, but rather to join the ranks of those speedy super-mamas that maintain a fit and fast pregnancy and set a marathon PR only a few months after delivery. I was definitely not abandoning caution, however; my little one's health was my first priority, and I only intended to continue the same fitness regime I had been doing for years, reducing intensity and volume as necessary. Should be easy, right? After all, if all of those women could do it, so could I.

And run I did...for four months. Only four months into my pregnancy, and suddenly I couldn't run without intense pelvic pain. My son was a small baby - only 5lbs 5oz at birth - and I only gained 28lbs by the time I delivered, so at 4 months I was barely showing. Just before becoming pregnant, I had run a Boston-qualifying marathon time having trained with more intensity and mileage than I ever had before. I was in peak fitness, yet my pelvis couldn't take it. I was relegated to the elliptical for the remainder of my pregnancy, and then no cardio for the last month. My pregnancy otherwise went without a hitch – a stroke of luck for which I am so very grateful– but losing running just didn't seem fair. I had already registered for a marathon that would take place exactly seven months after Jack's due date.

Even so, the disappointment of not running was rapidly displaced with the excitement and anticipation of giving birth for the first time, and for the first time in years, training wasn't heavy on my mind. My sweet, amazing baby boy stole my heart and my running shoes. But a couple of months after he was born, when resuming my running became a possibility, postpartum impatience would drive me to the dreaded shadowlands of "too much, too soon."

During this time spent in athletic purgatory, I gleaned some information that I wish I knew while pregnant. As a ~~biology teacher~~ running addict, I seek to understand as much about my own physiology as possible, from evolutionary history to biochemistry, another endeavor I am sure that you and I have in common. What resulted is a compilation of established wisdom on women's running lore as well as various tidbits from a vague crossroads of anecdotes and academic study. As loose as it may sound, the latter is important. Since pregnant women are rarely used as test subjects of rigorous scientific study, anecdotal information is often the only information, and because no two initiations into mommy-hood are alike, the best ways we can help each other is to share our own experiences.

Because of its emphasis on competitive running, this book is likely to be most useful to competitive runners, elite and sub-elite. That is certainly *not* to say that non-competitive runners won't also benefit from or enjoy the read! No matter what motivates you to lace up those trainers and skip out the door, all of us experience a change in our running lives when we become mothers. No matter how diverse those changes are, they are guaranteed to sometimes throw us for physical, mental, and emotional loops. Embrace them, and bring them with you as you read.

I want you to laugh, to cry, to know that whatever fears or running troubles brought you to this book, you are not alone. And you will continue to be the speedy, powerful warrior you always envisioned. You can be faster! Now with an even more amazing "personal best" in your life: a happy and healthy family. It's time to open up to each other about this ultimate of challenges.

Who's with me?

PART I – YOU RUNNING

"If you are losing faith in human nature, go out and watch a marathon." – Kathrine Switzer

Chapter 1
Why Do We Run?

It's 5:00 in the morning. Your alarm goes off, or if you're like me, your toddler has been awake and babbling for at least fifteen minutes already. This alarm was *your* doing. Yet your whole body cringes at the sound of it, and you likely utter some variety of expletives, either out loud or just in your groggy head. Every fiber of your being tries to get you to stay in bed.

Just a few more minutes.

Just make today your rest day and run tomorrow.

Just run in the afternoon instead.

It is a persistent force, that brain of yours. Yet something else is more relentless. A stronger drive wins out. A part of you that set the alarm clock in the first place, after checking your training schedule the night before. The training schedule that you (or your coach, if you have one) once meticulously poured over, for hours. And enjoyed it. The part of you that passed on wine during dinner knowing the morning workout that awaited you. The part of you that set your running clothes out the night before to make the hardest part of running – getting your butt out the door – just a little more seamless (clothing…seamless…this is not the only bad pun you'll read).

There they are, your running clothes, staring you down in the glow of your wailing alarm clock. It's starting to come back to you now, the strong part of you, slowly overtaking the excuses. Now you are up. And once your shoes are tied, your music on, your GPS watch aglow and standing by, you step into the darkness. One or two deep breaths and you're fueled with potential. The potential to make yourself just that much faster, stronger, happier, and healthier.

We are the rulers of the early morning, pushing the world along beneath our feet. We see our towns and cities in a way that most never will. We arrive at work with a certain spark after a successful workout just an hour or so before. When our legs hit us with a sharp reminder of the work we put them through as we try to stand or sit, we feel a smile behind the cringe, relishing every element of the challenge of training. When our friends, family, or colleagues ask us what time we got up to run, or how far we ran, we answer with genuine humility. Because despite their reactions – *Why would you get up THAT early to RUN? I could never do that* – and despite the pre-alarm clock voice in our heads that wins out over most people, this lifestyle is not so radical to us. It is simply what we must do.

But why? Why must we?

Chances are, your answer to this question will change throughout your life. Maybe you took up running to lose weight and are now racing at USATF national championships. Or perhaps you started running just on the weekends to gain fitness for another sport, and now travel the world running ultramarathons.

Whatever your reason, you are part of a rapidly growing tribe. More and more people are taking up running as a hobby. Specifically, more and more women. And more runners are choosing to be competitive athletes every year. RunningUSA reports that as of 2013, the number of race-finishing runners had increased around 300% since 1990, and the female percentage of those runners has risen from 25% to 57% over the same time period.[1] That's right, we are more than half the field! And it was only 43 years ago that women were first allowed to run the Boston Marathon. Our sisterhood is becoming unstoppable.

What draws each of us to running varies pretty considerably. Lifestyle change for health is likely the most common reason among non-competitive runners, or at least those who started off that way. A strong and attractive physique is certainly a big draw, a reward that running very efficiently provides. I've heard friends and acquaintances say something

---

[1] Statistics from the 2014 State of the Sport – Part III US Race Trends by RunningUSA, published July 9 2014

to the effect of "I run so I can eat." Fair enough. Running camaraderie is a wonderful draw for many; an instant family in exchange for miles. Many people feel that running clears their minds and stabilizes them emotionally, which has certainly been proven true in science and anecdote. Just ask our spouses what we are like when we are unable to run. For an increasing number of us, running takes an even deeper role: a means of uncovering our greatest selves, an arena for perpetual self-improvement.

When I had just moved to the Central Coast of California, I was registered to run in the Nike Women's Marathon in San Francisco. Nike was doing a pre-race media campaign asking registrants to fill in the blank: *I run to be_____*. This mantra would then go on a Nike t-shirt or wristband. The list of responses was long, often creative or humorous. *Strong. Fast. A badass. Eating. Fit. Beautiful. Stress-free. Free. Happy. Injured. Healthy. Less crazy. Not fat. Alive. Moving.* I never could come up with just one or two words to describe what running makes me into. At that point in my life, I didn't really know where my running would take me, beyond wanting to qualify for Boston. I knew I ran to be *something*, but couldn't formulate exactly what that was, or will be. Leaving it blank seemed like the best answer. I'm glad I did. My journey with running has recently taken me to places I couldn't have imagined, uncovering parts of myself I hadn't met yet.

Maybe you have your answer to the question. Maybe you've had to verbalize it every time your non-running friends and family question your sanity for willingly doing what they only did as punishment in high school PE class. Maybe, like me, you can't quite put words to it. Or maybe running is so ingrained in your being that you haven't ever thought about it.

If you are about to become a parent, now is the time to really think about why you run. Think of it as a statement of purpose. The fastest American female marathoner, and mother of four-year-old Piper, Deena Kastor, reflects on the importance of "purpose":

"Your purpose may be different than before you were pregnant. Defining why you run is different from a goal. I previously ran to get the best performance out of myself and now I run to be an example for my

daughter to joyfully follow her passions. **Purpose is different than a goal.** *Maybe your goal is to qualify for the Olympic Trials, but asking yourself* ***why*** *connects you to a deeper* ***purpose.***"[2]

This is not to say that changing your purpose diminishes or lessens goals you once had. Remember, goals are not the same as purpose, and you may very well reach those same goals under a different purpose.

But the changes in your life may have changed your internal drive, and in order to reach your goals – old or new – it is crucial to get in touch with that deeper purpose. Perhaps ask yourself the following questions:

What does it do for me?

What role does it have in my life?

Where do I want to go with my running?

Take some time to really explore these questions, and then write down your personal "statement of purpose". This is such an important part of your growth as a mother-runner, which is why I am discussing it early in the book. It starts with coming to grips with one critical fact:

However your children enter your lives, through birth or marriage or adoption, becoming a parent WILL change your running.

As scary as this may seem, it is not always a bad thing. But because most of us competitive runners – I'm going to say around 110%, give or take a few – are control freaks, the idea of our running lives being altered in incalculable ways is incredibly unnerving. You have big running goals for yourself. You envision your training and racing as a consistent progression, all of which is determined by your meticulous research, planning, and execution of your training. Your mantra is "the harder I work, the luckier I get." Even your adaptability is planned as necessary deviations from training arise. If you've been running and racing hard for at least a few years, you've learned that adaptability is a variable just as crucial to your running success as proper footwear, supportive bras, and anti-chafe clothing.

---

[2] Read more about Deena's experience with pregnancy and training at the end of Chapter 2.

Let me tell you, soon-to-be momma runners: you are about to set some huge PRs in adaptability.

And just that, itself, will change your running for the better.

Chapter 2
Why Don't We Run?

Ha, nope. We run.

Seriously, though, sometimes we have to not run. This is a dark time for us all. And a very confusing time for our family and friends who love us and support us no matter what flavor of crazy we manifest while not running.

Maybe you have had to take significant time off of training before for injury or illness, and if so, you've witnessed for yourself that your non-running condition is not permanent, that you most likely don't lose as much fitness as you think you will and that your life *DOES* go on. Consciously, intellectually, we know this. Yet we cannot help but live in fear that our hard-earned speed will go the wayside. And sometimes that is when we make bad decisions about our training.

Selective memory

My mom grew up in the bush of Alaska, where she had a feisty terrier named Fritz. She has told me several times of Fritz's many unfortunate encounters with porcupines, and the long, tedious process of removing hundreds of quills from the poor dog's face. You would think that after the first or second time this has happened, Fritz would remember the excruciating pain inflicted upon him and think twice about messing with porcupines when he saw them again. But many more porcupine incidents ensued during his lifetime. Whenever Fritz saw a porcupine, rather than remembering the pain, he was overpowered by a need for revenge and charged the spiny creature with even more gusto than the time before. The porcupine always won.

We do this when injuries creep up on us: selective memory. Rather than remember how we tried running through pain before and wound up injured for much longer than if we had heeded our bodies' signals, or how we finally *did* rebound from an injury stronger and faster than we were before, we only think of how much it would suck to lose our hard-earned fitness. And then we ignore warning signs, make excuses for what's causing our pain, and try to run through it. And we get quilled *every time we do this*. Why? Because we fear not running more than we fear injury. Yet we don't handle injury well when it does strike.

Selective memory can really be a double-edged sword, too. If you've given birth before, think of how powerfully it applies to new motherhood. We very quickly forget the pain of labor and childbirth, regardless of how we may have felt or what thoughts went through our heads during excruciating pain. We remember the intense joy, falling in love with our beautiful babies and relish those first photos and memories for years to come. We are hard-wired that way; our species may have gone extinct long ago if we remembered *everything*. It is nature's way of saying "wasn't that awesome?! Now get out there and do it again, champ."

Make no mistake, though, nature is also fickle. While reveling in our speedy mile repeats, we may not always remember what that inflamed IT band or strained piriformis muscle felt like, but that is not our body's invitation to take a "balls to the wall" approach in training. Our body's cues to ease back are often much more subtle and can even speak a different language entirely during pregnancy.

The bottom line, friends: sometimes we have to take a break from running.

Many running mamas choose to take time off from running while pregnant and use it as a chance to let their running bodies recover from years of intense training, enjoy a different fitness activity, or let their minds and hearts get preoccupied with a glorious new adventure. These are *all* excellent reasons to take a break from running during pregnancy. It may actually come as a welcome break, but even if not, some downtime can benefit your running just as much as it will your pregnancy. But it is crucial that you understand that, both pre and post-pregnancy, the biggest risk to your future as a runner is failure to recognize how your body is changing, and to try to come back to your prior running fitness too soon.

To train, or not to train

When my husband and I decided we wanted to have a baby, we started thinking about the timeliness of the process. We probably did TOO much thinking about it. I wanted to qualify for Boston first, train through my pregnancy as much as possible, and then race another marathon within the first year of baby's birth. I was a complete control freak about it and even got worried about my fertility following marathon training. As it happened, no less than two months after I squeaked out a BQ at the California International Marathon, we found out that were expecting. We counted our blessings that we conceived so quickly and commenced extreme excitement.

Obviously, I wanted to know as much as possible about my running during pregnancy. My doctor recited the accepted approach that I could carry on with the caliber of training I was accustomed to, but to back off as my body dictates. Everything I read on the internet reflected this advice.

I don't remember consciously deciding that I would train through my pregnancy. It was simply a given, in my mind, and my plans followed. But you know what they say about the best-made plans. I was conscientious of my body's changes, and just at the start of the second trimester, it spoke loud and clear that running was not going to continue. Pelvic pain ensued with every step, and training halted.

Because the decision to train through pregnancy was a no-brainer for me, I assumed that all other serious runners were doing the same. I felt like a failure, a weak runner who was going to lose everything I had worked for, all the fitness gains, all of my endurance. If I saw a visibly pregnant runner while I was walking on the trail, pangs of jealously flowed through me. *Why can she do it, but I can't?*

Maybe you have been in this situation yourself. Maybe you couldn't run through your first pregnancy, or you did run through your first and are suddenly stumped that you can't run through your second or third. You assume a downward progression of your athletic life, especially as you mature and imagine a ticking clock on your athletic career.

Good news: there are two flaws in our thinking.

The first is that everyone else is successfully training through their pregnancies. Many other runners find themselves in the same situation as I was in. They start out with iron-clad training plans and their bodies promptly melt that iron down with the inevitable – and amazing – changes pregnancy brings.

The second misconception we tend to harbor is that all serious, competitive runners should choose to train through their pregnancies. For some, pregnancy serves as a much-needed break from serious training and time for recovery. This does not diminish your future as a runner! Believe it or not, your body can, and will, rebound better than you probably think. Muscle memory and cumulative endurance capacity are amazing things. Plus, during that non-running time, your body may repair functional problems or near-injuries that you didn't even know were there. This is actually one component of how many runners rebound stronger and faster after pregnancy.

If there is one thing I truly regret about my pregnancy, is it spending a single second of it in resentment of the fact that I couldn't run. I had raced five marathons and will likely race dozens more in my lifetime, but how many times was I going to experience the incredible process of pregnancy?

I certainly am not here to advocate training through your pregnancy or not training through your pregnancy. That decision is yours and yours alone. I do, however, want to emphasize that this decision will *not* make or break your future as a runner, but if you're uptight about deviating from training plans, it might make or break the wholeness you feel during your pregnancy. Nine-plus months is a blink-of-an-eye in the course of your life, and in the endurance running world. Whatever you decide to do, whatever your body decides you will do, relish in your pregnancy!

Training may serve as a powerful part of that joy, showing you a new side of running and challenging you in a unique way. Or training may have no place in this new physiological dynamic, leading you to discover a new, awesome activity that you otherwise would not have sought out. As you plot a course through your pregnancy, embrace the "off-roading" that your body may take you through. When you read the "Mighty Mamas" stories, you will see such a richness of variety in the pregnancy-running experience, and hopefully that will inspire your own philosophy.

Whatever you decide to do, make sure that "joy" is your primary training goal.

Mighty Mama: Deena Kastor

Age: 42

Home: Mammoth Lakes, CA

Profession / Run Life: Elite runner for Asics, 2008 Olympic marathon bronze medalist, American record holder in the marathon, half-marathon, road 15K, road 8K, and road 5K.

Children: Daughter, Piper, born February 2011

What about your pregnancy surprised you, in terms of how your training was affected?

I was training for the NY marathon when I found out we were pregnant. I immediately shifted my goal from winning that race to creating a healthy child. It was almost instinctual to go from a selfish goal to a nurturing one, but in there I thought running had a place. I decided I would run 30-45 minutes every day simply to be healthy. I wasn't going to train, but I would run for the health of my child's and my body and mind. It didn't take long to get the greatest lesson pregnancy and motherhood would teach me, flexibility. I had awful side stitches when I ran. Soon after I had awful side stitches when I even walked the dog. So, I did the only things that my body felt good doing, deep cleaning the house, cooking and reading. It wasn't a difficult choice because I wanted to feel good physically and emotionally for the development of Piper.

How long after delivery did it take for your "training groove" to return?

So, after 5 months of being sedentary I gave birth to Piper via C-section which was another lesson in flexibility because it was far from my plan. It was only 2 weeks after she was born that we were in the midst of another snow storm and I was on the treadmill walking with her in my arms and using an exaggerated bounce to lull her to sleep (my husband's tactic was walking 100 flights of our stairs). When she finally fell asleep I asked Andrew to take her because I felt the urge to run. I increased the speed of the treadmill and broke into a jog. It felt SO GOOD! I still had stitches in, but the flow and tingle of my blood moving through me—despite the fact that it was only 3.5 miles an hour—was so exhilarating. When I was pregnant, I didn't put pressure on myself to come back and run. I had no idea what motherhood was about or if my passion for running would re-ignite. It did. Thanks to so many mothers before me who showed that you could balance running, careers and a family I set out to do it myself.

What part of your training was modified the most, both pre and postpartum?

The part that modified most was less sleep. I made a conscious decision to cut some of my miles because I wasn't getting afternoon naps in. Piper—she is my child after all—is a great sleeper even at 4 years old with 3 hour naps and 10 hour nights, but I use her nap time to give interviews, catch up on emails and prep dinner.

Did you battle with any lingering injuries in the months/years following pregnancy?

I came back from pregnancy very slow. It wasn't until a month of running and building to about an hour that I finally put on a watch. A

GPS wasn't the best choice since the reality of my pace was slow and shocking. I think a big difference is a vaginal birth versus C-section. With natural births you get a pelvic shift and elasticity that your body needs to get used to. A <u>slow</u> and <u>mindful</u> comeback is always going to work in your favor. Much of the time in training I try to ignore aches and pains, trying to rise above them, but post-partum is a grand exception.

Do you breastfeed? If so, how has that impacted your training?

I did breast feed for 6 months. I have always focused on nutrition and this seemed the ideal way to feed, but this was another lesson in flexibility. I wanted to breast feed for an entire year but realized that I wasn't producing enough and needed to supplement with formula after 3 months. I was upset with myself for not being able to naturally provide the nutrients my daughter needed and soon realized I needed to cut my perfectionist expectations. It was a moment of clarity that her birth didn't go naturally like I wanted so I wanted to make up for it by breastfeeding the first year only to alter my ideals once again. Breast feeding didn't impact my training with the exception of the day I leaked through my shirt when a baby was crying at the park I was doing mile repeats. Ooops!

Any specific tips on staying healthy / injury free that you recommend for competitive new mamas?

Always run with caution when running post-pregnancy. Our bodies go through such a physical and hormonal shift that it needs time to adjust and strengthen. It is also important to define why you run. Your purpose may be different than before you were pregnant. Defining why you run is different from a goal. I previously ran to get the best performance out of myself and now I run to be an example for my daughter to joyfully follow her passions. Purpose if different than a goal. Maybe your goal is to qualify for the Olympic Trials, but asking yourself why connects you to a deeper purpose.

How did you cope with sleepless nights, time constraints, and work schedules in those early new baby months?

Lack of sleep is life's greatest torture. I'm not sure I coped with it, but I remember telling my husband that the exhaustion I felt was greater than hitting the wall in the marathon. And speaking of my husband, Andrew *was significant in our new role as parents. I remember breast feeding at 3am and him, eyes half-opened, coming out of the bedroom asking wearily if I needed anything. French toast. I was starving, so at 3am, my husband fired up the cast iron skillet and got busy prepping us breakfast.*

Has your relationship with competitive running changed since becoming a parent? If so, how?

My purpose is different. I want to be a good role model for Piper. I want her to see Andrew and I joyously following our passions, having goals, committing, working hard, achieving goals, falling short and all the while having a ball.

Chapter 3
Building Your Team

As you know, if you have ever coached track or cross country, running sports can often be perceived as a training tool to enhance performance in other sports, or as a catch-all for the lanky kids with poor hand-eye coordination. I can't count the number of times a parent has said "Well can't [kid's name] do [other sport] and cross country this fall? Since it's an individual sport, they can train on their own and not come to practice."

I can safely attribute the poor condition of my molars to my habit of discretely grinding them whenever someone utters the phrase *"it's just an individual sport"*. As if that means it requires less training and focus than a sport in which a ball is constantly passed between players. Every so often, ESPN, Sportology, and a variety of other sports literature publishes a list of "Top Ten Most Difficult Sports." Even though there is not a scientific metric for 'hardness' of athletic activity, and the lists are really just subjective opinions of the authors, it is worth noting that *every single time* the lists have included the following: track/cross country, wrestling, boxing, mixed martial arts, swimming, and gymnastics. All of these are considered 'individual sports'. So why, exactly, would they require *less* practice time and emphasis than sports with balls and nets? Why? WHY?!

I digress. Done with rant. The difficulty level of running sports as compared to others isn't my point. The more important thing here is that the notion that track and cross country are "individual sports" is actually incorrect. Every athlete's participation matters, in training and in competition, to both their successes as individuals and to the success of the team.

From a spectator's perspective, distance running races appear to be fairly uncomplicated and entirely individual. There isn't yelling between players, or (much) physical contact, or the display of some spectacular skill that sends "wows" through the crowd, at least not until a close battle at the finish line. To non-runners, it appears quiet, placid, and simple. Intense, but not aggressive. And that is the great illusion of running, because what is happening in the minds of the athletes couldn't be more radically different than it appears on the surface.

In a competitive race, there is intense nonverbal communication between runners, whether teammates or total strangers. You hang behind the leader's shoulder in the first mile, and she knows you are letting her "pull" the group. You decide to surge in the latter third of the race and others will try to float behind you. You drive hard on a steep uphill to lose the other frontrunners and they decide to hold steady and catch you on the downhill. Cross country and track runners get to know each other's paces, idiosyncrasies of their strides, and racing habits very, very well, so that they can best utilize their strengths *as a team* to earn points against the competition. They know which runners from other teams to really race hard against and which to ignore. They know how to leverage the weaknesses of their competitors on specific courses and conditions. And they are balancing all of this in their heads for the entire race, all the while fighting their own minds' attempts to get them to quit.

This is a sport of extreme mental strength, and of keen perceptive abilities. I might be preaching to the choir on this topic, but recognizing the team aspect of competitive running is crucial for improvement and long-term success in the sport. Because we competitive recreational runners do not usually belong to an official team, at least not in the collegiate sense, we tend to overlook the important benefits of team running.

Social animals
When asked what the best part of running is, many women refer to the camaraderie and friends they have made. It is a truly special and wonderful social experience! Those other early-morning (or late afternoon) track, trail, or road dwellers are your athletic soulmates. Once you start training with a buddy or a group, it is amazing how quickly you'll strike up common interests in conversation, vent about your training, and before you know it, you're regularly discussing details of your running life that you don't even share with your significant other. A runner friend of mine once said, "my running buddy knows more about my bodily

functions than my husband!" Such camaraderie is what motivates many women to improve and excel in their running.

If you are running while pregnant, particularly in the third trimester, there is another good reason to run with a buddy or in a group: the security of having someone nearby if you experience any pain, contractions, or otherwise need to stop. Most of us run with our cell phones on our person these days, so calling for help is fairly simple, but having a buddy with you does add a little peace of mind. Of course this all depends on where you run, how far from home, how close to bathrooms or water, and how your pregnancy has progressed.

Perhaps most importantly to new moms, running with a partner or group can bring you a very much needed social break from the new baby routine, bringing new and like-minded people into your life. Even the most independent of runners can often find ourselves feeling lonely and cut-off from in the new dynamic of motherhood, especially those of us who stop working full-time to stay home with the baby for a while. Getting out of the house and connecting with fellow runners can be a powerful mental and emotional boost, and it is cheaper than therapy.

Lone wolf

While the social element of group running is a big draw for some women, and certainly has its benefits, others prefer the solitary run life. Some fall somewhere in between, as I do. Perhaps you got into running because you enjoyed the time alone with your own thoughts, to meditate, to process, to discipline your mind along with your body. This, too, is one of the great joys and benefits of running. When you have kids at home, in particular, *any* alone time is to be treasured and protected like it's the Hope Diamond. Maybe time to tune into your favorite music, audiobook, or podcast, or perhaps some pure and simple quiet.

When I was pregnant with my son, I was living and teaching at an all-girls boarding school. While I loved my job there and greatly enjoyed living in a vibrant school community, like other faculty and staff, my attention was in high-demand, at all times. For better or for worse, there was no separation between my personal and professional life. Getting off campus for a run – pre-pregnancy, in the few months of my pregnancy when I *could* run, and postpartum - was a perfect dose of "me-time." And, admittedly, a mood-improver. Endorphins rock.

The best of both worlds

So which is better? Flying solo or teaming up? On one hand, some quality "me time" is sacred under new-mommyhood circumstances. On the other hand, expanding the scope of your world can help with your sanity and perspective. You don't have to choose. You can have a little bit of both if you want the benefits of both.

Whether or not you decide to run with a team or group, it is a generally accepted fact that if you want to get faster, you probably should run with someone of comparable ability to your own, maybe just a tad faster. But it doesn't have to be all the time, every day. If you are strained for time during the work week and must seek out your workouts at inconsistent times, maybe meet with a group just once over the weekend. You certainly can benefit from less frequent – but consistent – group runs, which can provide a small stimulus to your easy pace and give even the most independent of minds a friendly conversation to break up the potential monotony of a long run.

Remember: your "team" can be anywhere and everywhere. It can be an official group that trains and competes together. It can be a gathering of friends who finish a leisurely run with a cold beer and laughs. It can be an exchange of tweets or Facebook messages. An experienced runner who works at your local running store and shares war stories and advice with you. It can even be a simple head-nod of acknowledgement that total strangers exchange on a run, a fleeting but poignant tip of solidarity that lends a boost during pouring rain, blistering heat, or the end of a long run. That quick glance or smile that says "Hey fellow runner! You rock." You know what look I am referring to.

Whether you are expecting or are a new mom, whether you prefer to run alone or with a group, you will benefit from engaging with your running 'team', and the local running community at large. If you're struggling with anything in your running life, anything at all, simply discovering that you are not alone can go a long, long way in lifting your spirits. You may need it more than you realize, and your baby will thank you for it!

Ok, maybe not literally. Kids won't thank you for most things, so time to get used to that. But you get the idea.

Your pit crew

Let us not ever forget the teammates we have at home and elsewhere in our lives. Our family and friends who have stood with cow bells at the finish of countless races. Our spouse who has relinquished uninterrupted sleep to hundreds or thousands of early morning alarms so that we can get our runs in before work. Our sports doctors who have had to reprimand us time and time again after we should have been resting. We are so fortunate to have this level of support as we pursue our favorite pastime. Let them know how much you appreciate it!

Pregnancy adds another member to this "You Team": the OBGYN. This is the first person to consult on the topic of running during and following your pregnancy. They will tell you if you are healthy enough to continue your current intensity and volume of training, or that you should scale back. In tracking baby's development through the pregnancy, they will tell you if your level of activity could negatively impact baby's growth. Chances are, if your pregnancy is uncomplicated, this will not be an issue for you.

With baby on the way, this is an important time to rally your team. Talk with your spouse, family, and doctor about your running goals. Have a plan, but be ready to throw the plan out the window if your body demands it. Your running will be all the better because you have a support crew!

The Oiselle Volée Team

Your team can even be a long-distance relationship made possible by social media technology. I was very fortunate to gain an incredible "team" in this way by joining Oiselle's ambassador team, Volée. If you haven't heard of them, Oiselle (French for "female bird") is an amazing women's running clothing company out of Seattle, growing rapidly in the athletic apparel world as an underdog to juggernauts like Nike (but have signed former Nike athletes and superwomen, Lauren Fleshman and Kara Goucher).

Volée (French for "flock") is an extension of their racing teams. For an annual membership fee, members receive a racing singlet, merchandise perks, and best of all, an incredible community of like-minded women. Volée members get together for runs and races, promote women's running in their local communities, and support each other through means including Strava, Twitter, and Facebook. As an introvert who tends to keep few, close friends, social media was not exactly my cup of tea. I didn't have a Twitter or Strava account prior to joining. But besides being a fan of Oiselle's clothing, I was still drawn to the team concept they had created.

As soon as I became a member and created a Twitter handle, I was flooded with tweets of welcome and encouragement from women all over the country. Those who live in my state were ecstatic to have another teammate in their vicinity. We communicate over all things running, whether we had a bad workout and need a shout-out, or are struggling with mid-run digestive woes, or are battling through the injury blues, or just had the race of a lifetime. This instant sisterhood has been a tremendously positive force in my running life, far more so that I expected it to be. A uniquely successful way to connect with and define 'team'.

Chapter 4
Setting Goals

I have found there to be only one certainty in running: if you stick with it long enough, running improves you. This happens when we are challenged, not when everything is copacetic. It happens during any and all points of our lives, even during the middle of adulthood when we may feel that our growth has stagnated. When we set goals for ourselves, we are projecting our desire for this growth into a tangible object on the horizon. The challenge is plotting the course to reach it. If you have established a "statement of purpose", as we discussed in Chapter 1, you've got yourself a compass!

Great expectations

In my time coaching high school cross country and track, I am always impressed by how the kids on my team mature and progress during their four or more years of training and racing. They first come out for the team as gawky, and often self-described "nerdy", eighth and ninth graders who struggle to figure out how to use this ever-changing and confusing body of theirs. We the coaches push them to use it in a controlled, disciplined manner that advances their training goals, whether or not they know exactly what their goals are.

This is no easy task, and can come with great frustration for all involved. Some have competed in other sports before, others have taken up running specifically because they have *not* succeeded at other sports. Some come bursting with enthusiasm to continue their favorite activity, and others only came out for the team because their parents made them. It's always a menagerie, and successfully executing a structured workout for these youngsters can often feel like herding cats. But with patience on our part, over the course of four years we coaches are overjoyed to witness these youngsters' running form evolve from a lopsided windmill to a smooth, efficient gazelle, and their ability to focus go from Jar-Jar Binks to Obi-Wan Kenobi.[3]

---

[3] It is worth pointing out that only coaches of track / cross country would make a

The key to their success is setting goals that are appropriate to both their *individual fitness levels* and their *trainability,* how well they respond to the demands of training. Not only must the goal setting and training plan take into account the many demands on their time as student-athletes, as well as the complex body changes they are going through, it must challenge them, but also be close enough for them to reach out and touch. A thirteen year old rookie runner shouldn't expect to run as fast as the varsity captain during her first year, but should be thrilled to see her 5K time drop from 28 minutes to 25 minutes by the end of the season, and recognize that she can improve in future years with continued focus and dedication to her training.

So, mama, what does this have to do with your running?

Just as novice athletes sometimes set unrealistically high expectations – their "eyes are faster than their legs", as I like to say – those of us fiercely competitive runners often do the same thing when our training hits a speed bump….a baby bump, in this case! Don't get me wrong, it is <u>good</u> to set goals for ourselves in lieu of injury, pregnancy, or another break from training. But we have to be mindful in tempering our drive to continue getting faster and the needs of our bodies.

Tune in, first, to your *purpose,* as you hopefully identified in Chapter 1.

Then consider goals that manifest that purpose.

This might mean taking a very different approach to training than you had pre-pregnancy, even towards the same goal. Maybe before you had successfully completed four half-marathons using a 12-week training plan, but now you need to take 18 weeks to ensure your body is ready to tackle the same task. Maybe you were healthfully running 75 miles per week preparing for your last marathon, but with a new infant in the house waking you up every three hours at night, you'll need to scale back to maxing out at 60 miles per week to avoid overtraining. Maybe you still want to qualify for Boston, just as you did before pregnancy, but this time your schedule only allows you to train four days a week instead of six.

Star Wars reference in regards to anything athletic.

Maybe your body isn't as eager to continue training during your pregnancy as your mind is, and you need to take a break.

The good news is that if you do decide (or your body forces you) to scale back your training volume or intensity, you will ultimately *most likely* perform better than you *think* you will. During pregnancy, if you choose to race, performance necessarily takes a back seat. But as we will discuss in later chapters, you can potentially experience an *increase* in VO2 max up to around a year after giving birth. How much this changes does, of course, vary significantly from person to person, but every little bit helps.

Just keep your purpose in focus, and prioritize the long-term over the short-term. You may have to take one or two steps back in order to take three or four steps forward. Consider how much the teenage athletes can improve over the course of a few meager years, time which feels like a drop in the bucket of our lifetimes when we are more mature, and begin cultivating patience. Yes, you are older than the teenage athletes, and your lifestyle is radically different, but you also, most likely, have more years of competitive running under your belt. Your muscles, joints, tendons, and brain are conditioned for this. Your body *will* remember.

Journaling the journey

Some people keep journals. They have written a reflection every day since they could write, and by the time they are thirty have volumes upon volumes of journals filled with their daily musings. Many of these people become excellent writers and speakers for their honed introspective skills. I remember how keeping a diary or journal was always recommended and sometimes required in grade school, and continues to be recommended in a spectrum of career choices. There are advantages to looking back at past thoughts, but also great value in successfully verbalizing your thoughts as they come. I admire journal-keepers for their disciplined documenting regimen.

Until recently I had always struggled with keeping a journal. Remembering to journal was most of the battle, and feeling inspired to write after an exhausting day was another. When blogging became a 'thing' (anyone remember LiveJournal?) I made a solid attempt at keeping a regular blog. But this fell the wayside too. The only time I finally got myself to keep a daily journal was when my now-husband and I were in a long-distance relationship. We created a private blog that we used to write each other love letters at the end of every day, a way to feel a different kind of closeness that doesn't always come through on phone calls or Skype sessions. Writing does that: brings out a different part of oneself, often times a deeper part. So I could journal for him, but couldn't ever seem to journal just for me.

That is, of course, until I started keeping a running journal.

I had always mapped out my training plans, of course, but had not documented my training retrospectively. I was consistently a healthy runner and rarely experienced stomach distress during my runs, so I never really felt the need to track the fine details. But after my pregnancy, when injury and hormonal changes spun what I thought I knew about my body into a cyclone, I decided to keep a running journal to better get to know this new athlete that had taken over. The things I documented included:

The runs: distance and effort

Cross training: type and duration

Mood that day

How much sleep the night before

GI issues and possible food culprits

Something I chose not to include but is also widely considered worthwhile is a food journal. I opted not to because I personally don't struggle with GI distress very intensely or frequently, and passionately hate tracking food. But it is a great tool for many runners to overcome the dreaded runner's trots, cramps, and worse. There is a whole spectrum of other things worth documenting as well, depending on the individual.

When it was released in early 2015, I purchased the _Believe_ running journal by pros Lauren Fleshman and Roisin McGettigan-Dumas. This journal feels like more of a workbook: few blank pages and very fun and imaginative activities that foster self-reflection as well as quotes, quizzes, tips, and more. I really love this about it, though some folks prefer clean, clear pages to make their own without someone else's head in it too.

Totally make sense. For those who wish to journal, they should all find a format that best fits them.

The single most helpful thing about my running journal thus far is how it can serve as an "objective outsider" when I need it to. When the perils of overtraining are creeping up on me, and I try to wish away the symptoms with grit and stubbornness, I force myself to look back at the last couple of weeks and put together my training paces, sleep quality, mood, and overall impressions from the runs. When they show some deterioration, I know I am on thin ice. This is assuming, of course, that my journal entries have been as detailed and honest as possible.

One benefit of keeping a running journal is the ability to reflect on how the many facets of your training impact each other and find trends. Putting together all the pieces that comprise "you", the runner. Every little piece helps you to understand the short-term changes you go through from week to week that ultimately shape your training. Find out what holds you back from achieving your running goals, whether they are day-to-day workout goals or race times. There are also, of course, factors that shape your long-term growth.

Tips on goal-setting for expecting & new moms

Be honest about what you want out of running.

Consider the recent changes in your life and how running will fit differently into your schedule.

Be aware of your local running community – groups, teams, and races – and don't be afraid to reach out.

Baby steps, at first. Be patient!

Don't try to fit too rigidly into a cookie-cutter training plan. Be flexible!

If you haven't kept a running journal in the past, start keeping one.

Mighty Mama: Michelle Baxter

Age: 32

Home: Anchorage AK

Profession: Associate at The Skinny Raven (running store) & running blogger, www.therunnersplate.com

Run Life: Boston Marathon qualifier, frequent local age group and overall female winner

Children: Son, Cullen, born October 24th 2014.

During the first trimester I had NO motivation to run, which has never happened before. And when I got done with a run, I didn't have the runner's high like I usually do. I also had pain in my pelvis for some time. ART (active release therapy) helped solve that. I also had issues with my back and hip flexors. Most of the time the chiropractor was able to help through manual adjustments and ART.

What about your pregnancy surprised you, in terms of how your training was affected?

When I found out I was pregnant, my goal was to stay as active as possible and try to maintain as much fitness as I could. I was surprised that during the first trimester I had absolutely no motivation to run and no runner's high after finishing my run. It wasn't like me! I had always wanted to go out for a run and loved experiencing the runner's high afterwards. I expected to be slower and for my jog to turn into a waddle, but I actually didn't feel like I slowed down that much. My pace dropped 30- 45 seconds per mile, but I was actually still able to run some decent times when racing. I was also surprised that my belly didn't feel like it was bouncing while I was running. I expected that I would feel my baby bouncing up and down during the whole run, but it was actually quite firm. I did significantly cut back on my mileage. The previous summer I peaked at 100 miles during one week, but during my pregnancy my weekly mileage averaged 34 for the 1st trimester and just 13 miles per week during the 3rd trimester.

How long after delivery did it take for your "training groove" to return?

I started to walk/run 4 week postpartum. There was a lot of walking at first and very little running. I really started to feel better 3 months postpartum. During those first couple months of running, my C-section incision really bothered me, but then I started massaging the scar tissue and the pain went away. I was surprised I had very little desire to run the first month after having my son, but once the hormones evened back out, I was ready to run.

What part of your training was modified the most, both pre and postpartum?

During my pregnancy I really cut back on mileage and eventually had a hard time doing speed of any sort. During the 3rd trimester I only averaged 13 miles a week and was taking a lot of walk breaks during these runs.

Did you battle with any lingering injuries in the months/years following pregnancy?

No, thankfully I feel great these days! (6 months postpartum at this time) I have been diligent about lifting weights twice a week, taking pilates and yoga to build my core back up, and trying to eat right and recover properly.

How has breastfeeding impacted your training?

Thankfully it hasn't impacted it at all. Well, except the fact I have to get up 15 minutes earlier in order to pump and/or nurse. And I've had to buy new sports bras because my old ones were just too small or not supportive enough.

Any specific tips on staying healthy / injury free that you recommend for competitive new mamas?

You've probably heard it time and time again, but listen to your body. Just like all of the new advice you are receiving on how to raise your baby, not all of it is the right advice for you. Consult other runner friends who have had children. Stay on top of hydrating and fueling properly for yourself and to maintain a solid milk supply (if you are breastfeeding). Don't think you can't be competitive anymore! I've found that I still want it as much as I did before I had my son, and I honestly believe I am going to set some PRs this summer!

How did you cope with sleepless nights, time constraints, and work schedules in those early new baby months?

I laid out my running plan, so I was only getting up early twice a week. (Prior to the baby, I would get up every single morning at 5:00/5:30 a.m. to run, but I knew that might not be very feasible with a newborn.) I would one run on the treadmill while my baby played beside me or while he was at the gym child care facility. The other workouts were done either when my husband got home from work or on the weekend. I also make sure to coordinate with my husband's schedule in advance so I don't miss any workouts. I try to go to bed as soon as (or shortly after) my son goes to bed, then at least I can get some sleep, even if it is broken sleep.

Has your relationship with competitive running changed since becoming a parent? If so, how?

Not really. I am still super competitive about my running and might even 'want it' more now because I want to prove myself as a new momma!

PART II – YOU EXPECTING

"To be pregnant is to be vitally alive, thoroughly woman, and distressingly inhabited. Soul and spirit are stretched – along with body – making pregnancy a time of transition, growth, and profound beginnings." – Anne Christian Buchanan

Chapter 5
Your Pregnant Running Body: The Basics

Here in "The West", it wasn't too long ago that women were highly discouraged from doing *any* physical exercise during pregnancy, let alone a high-impact activity like running. Even being out in public while pregnant had been restrained; that is a thing of the past for most Western cultures but is still practiced in others. Reading nineteenth or eighteenth century classic literature you hear pregnant women described as "ill with child", as if it were a disease, a necessary but unsightly bane in society that required them to be tucked away as soon as their pregnancies became visible.

It is certainly true that pregnancy has the potential to serve up an assortment of complications, particularly for women who do not have access to adequate maternal health care. Some would argue that medical involvement is unnecessary and even harmful since humanoid women have been giving birth successfully for millions of years without hospitals or doctors involved. Others would argue that, yes they did, but a much higher percentage of them died in the process, as compared to today's maternal mortality rates with medical care.

Establishing the "best way" for women to be pregnant and give birth is a hotly debated topic these days, and looking to our ancestors for guidance can be a double-edged sword. But with respect to running and pregnancy, there is one glaring point that many momma-runners have pointed out:

If running caused damage to pregnancies, our species would definitely be extinct.

Our great, great, great...[insert many greats]...grandmothers, whether early *Homo sapiens* or *Homo habilis* or some of the earlier hominids had to outrun predators, chase down their other children, participate in hunting/gathering, all while pregnant. Ok, I'll grant that they likely got *some* reprise from hunting duties during the latter stages of pregnancy. Really, it makes no evolutionary sense at all for pregnancy to require that *any* mobile species be sedentary for the healthy birth and survival of the offspring. In today's world, most women are very fortunate today that when a woman is put on maternal bedrest, they will not risk malnutrition or starvation or attack by predators, though many do face other risks due to poor health care access.[4]

The point, though, is that exercise while pregnant is not only losing the stigma as a risk to mom and baby's health but has also been shown to be beneficial to both! That is, of course, assuming a low-risk pregnancy. It is always important to discuss your physical activities with your doctor to ensure that there aren't precautions you need to take, specific to your pregnancy, or that your particular activity has other possible risks. SCUBA diving, for example, is advised against because it puts the baby at risk of pressure-related complications. Full-contact sports, or activities with high risk of falling, are also advised against for pretty obvious reasons, so you might have to curb your desire for sky diving, rugby, cage fighting, or bull riding.

As for running, great news! It is generally considered safe, as long as you have a green light from your doctor. The prevailing wisdom today, according to the American College of Obstetricians & Gynecologists (ACOG), is that you can continue the level of exertion that your body is accustomed to, but to consult your doctor before beginning running for the first time.[5] Starting *any* new athletic activity puts your body under a new strain, with or without a baby inside it, so caution is warranted. At the same time, a previously sedentary women would greatly benefit – as would her baby – if she took up some regular, low-intensity exercise. The ACOG, as well as a myriad of other organizations, even encourage such exercise, as it helps mom to reduce stress, improve posture and muscle tone, improve sleep, lower blood pressure, and even cope better with labor.

---

[4] Many women in the world today do not have access to adequate maternal health care, and in these regions, the material mortality rates can be fairly high. Nonprofits like *Every Mother Counts*, founded by Christy Turlington, work to provide maternal health care to women across the world and ensure that no mother dies due to lack of proper care.

[5] The ACOG puts out a publication of Frequently Asked Questions on the subject of pregnancy and exercise, with some excellent recommendations, as well as warning signs of potential related problems.

Running can obviously have a very positive impact on your pregnancy, and studies have shown that babies benefit too. A study from the journal *Epidemiology* showed that women who engaged in vigorous exercise during an uncomplicated pregnancy had lower instances of preterm birth – completely opposite to the notions of exercise from as recently as thirty-plus years ago. In addition, the *Journal of Pediatrics* reported in the mid-'90s that children of mothers who exercised during pregnancy had less body fat and performed better on IQ tests than children of mothers who didn't exercise. Yes, exercise, even intense exercise, is great for you and baby.[6]

Flipping the tables a bit, pregnancy can definitely have a big impact on your pace and times. Last summer, UC-Berkeley 800m superstar Alysia Montano made national headlines when she raced the 800m at 34 weeks pregnant. She commented to reporters that she had felt great in her training during pregnancy and had been very cautious to ensure her baby's health in the process. Her time in that race was about 35-seconds short of her personal best, and she came in dead last. But that did not deter her enthusiasm for what she had accomplished, nor that of the crowd cheering her through the finish.[7] Alysia delivered a perfectly healthy, full-term baby girl that August.

Training and competing during pregnancy can bring a new sense of accomplishment, but probably not personal bests. There are indeed undeniable changes to your body, no matter how fast you are! In the rest of this chapter, we will examine the basics of those changes more closely, starting from the ground – up. In Chapter 6, we will dig deeper "Beyond the Basics", assessing some of the more in-depth science on running while pregnant.

While reading, bear in mind that not every woman experiences all of these changes. They are just common occurrences, some of which might

---

[6] These studies were discussed in the *Runner's World Guide To Running & Pregnancy*, and can be found in greater detail in the references section of this book.
[7] USA Today reported on Montano's race that her doctors more than approved of her training and racing, they encouraged her to do so.

occur during your first pregnancy but not subsequent pregnancies, or vice versa. Every pregnancy is different, and a wild ride of its own. So strap in!

You, from the ground up

Feet

You may have heard that your feet might swell frequently during pregnancy. You may also have heard that your feet grow in shoe size during pregnancy, and stay that way. Both of these things can be true for many women. Swelling (edema) is due to increased fluid retention that is necessary for a healthy pregnancy as well as slightly inhibited blood return from extremities to the heart, from which poor circulation, in general, can ensue. When feet increase in shoe size, aside from swelling, it is due to the weakening of the arch and increased pronation. These changes are caused by weight gain, shifts in pelvic orientation, and changes in gait. It is unlikely that such changes will occur until the mid to latter part of the second trimester, at the earliest. Whatever fitness activities you plan on engaging in during your pregnancy, invest in some comfortable – and maybe slightly larger – shoes, for all occasions!

Knees & Legs

Knee pain can be another common ailment, and from pretty much the same factors causing foot changes: weight gain, pelvic shift, gait change. Because running is high-impact, knee pain can be an unfortunate problem that forces many women to stop running and, instead, switch to the elliptical machine or swimming. Those aren't bad options! In fact, they are the best options for replacing running when impact is a concern. Knee issues are more likely to manifest later in pregnancy as well, depending on the amount of weight gain and the mother's frame.

Additionally, the ever-growing belly changes a woman's center of gravity - as you'll see in Figure 2 shifting it forward. This can influence where and how you land during a running stride, and possibly put increased strain on muscles and tendons that you don't normally stress. For example: you typically land on your heels, but with your belly pulling your weight forward you now land on the ball of your foot or toes, making your shin muscles work harder, and likely a little sore. Or very sore.

Hips

Hip and pelvic discomfort are also of similar cause. But since the womb sits in the pelvis like a melon in a fruit bowl, the impact of running is certainly not the only cause of discomfort. From about the second trimester onward, there's the joy of round ligament pain. The round ligament attaches your hips to the front of your uterus (see Figure 1), kind of like bungee cords. As your uterus grows those ligaments stretch, sending little twinges of pain along the sides of your lower abdomen, sometimes when you twist or stand up or make a sudden move, other times completely randomly. It's usually not a severe or troubling pain, and not likely to have a major impact on exercise. But it is important to be aware that these ligaments – as well as other soft tissue in your hips and abdomen – are loosening and relatively unstable during the gestational months.

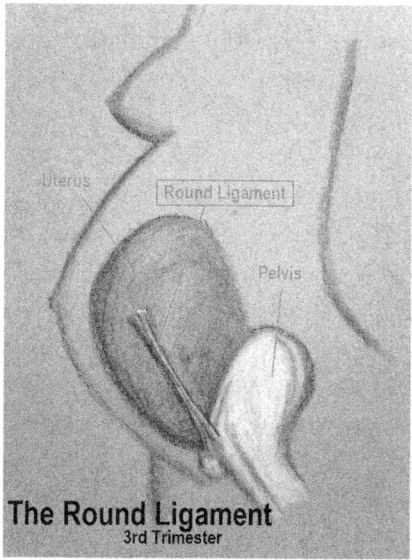

Figure 1- *The Round Ligament*

Then there are the hips themselves. Everyone has heard of "the waddle": the oh-so-wonderful gait attained by many women during the latter stages of pregnancy in which the pelvis has shifted to accommodate the growing belly, as well as the change in the woman's center of gravity (CG), and so the stride widens and accentuates a more side-to-side manner of walking. Not everyone experiences the waddle while pregnant since the degree of pelvic tilt depends greatly on the woman's build, weight, and belly size. Naturally, such changes will also affect running stride. Many women find that they are unable to continue running by the time they are in "full waddle" (towards the end of the third trimester) as the waddle itself indicates great difficulty in walking and maintaining a secure center of gravity. This is a time to be particularly cautious to avoid falling! Even if you are still doing intervals in your runs, the change in pelvic orientation and your shifted weight can throw off your usual rhythm at faster paces. It is recommended that you train on solid, even surfaces to avoid tripping, and ease gradually into your faster paces.

Belly
Ah, the belly. Site of the biggest pregnancy changes, inside and out. These changes may not be apparent early in pregnancy until that first bout of morning sickness during the first trimester. Make no mistake, morning sickness does *not* only strike in the morning, it can hit at any moment, anytime. While some women experience very little, others suffer to the max, with a small percentage even requiring hospitalization for it. The nausea has obvious effects on your running, so if you start to experience morning sickness on a run, take it easy, and hopefully get to the nearest bathroom. As you get to know your pregnant body more, you may find that running brings on the nausea, in which case you may need a little break. But fear not – most morning sickness subsides by the second trimester. Staying well hydrated is key, and if you are throwing up most of what you eat and drink, losing more water through sweat may not be the best idea. Everyone experiences morning sickness differently, and if you are experiencing it severely, do discuss it with your doctor.

Then there is the obvious expansion! As your belly grows in size, your center of gravity shifts forward. You can feel it when you run.

The larger you get, the greater the shift, so this is when you run a higher risk of losing your balance. To accommodate this shift, your stride may become wider and shorter, according to several studies on how pregnancy affects biomechanics.[8] Running on even terrain is advisable, and now isn't the time to try on a faster pace. Stick to what has been working thus far and what is familiar to you.

Back

As your belly grows in size, your hips and back undergo some changes to accommodate this new addition to your frame. This change has impacts all the way up your spine, as well, and is the main source of back pain during pregnancy. As your pelvis tilts forward, your lower (lumbar) vertebrae to curve slightly (see Figure 2). This makes the lower back muscles especially sensitive to strain and disks potentially prone to herniation. A good reason to be extra careful lifting objects. From your back's "perspective", running with a large belly is not too different from heavy lifting: during the take-off stage of your running stride, your back muscles contract to stabilize your body. Pregnant or not, you exert *three times your body weight* on your feet each time you land while running!

---

[8] One particular publication in BMC Pregnancy & Childbirth, **Trunk motion and gait characteristics of pregnant women when walking: report of a longitudinal study with a control group,** quantified this change in stride length and width, as well as how long it took to return to normal, prenatal measurements.

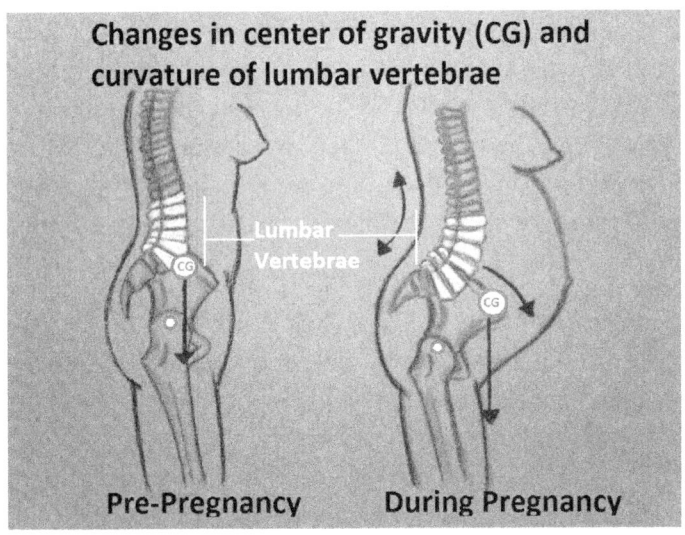

Figure 2 – *Center of gravity and spinal changes, both before and during pregnancy*

Many women have found that wearing a prenatal back brace when they exercise really helps to alleviate back and pelvic pain, providing a little bit of stability and keeping their belly from hammering down on the pelvis. It may or may not help with your discomfort, but is certainly worth a try.

Chest
Space comes at a premium in your body during pregnancy and things start to get crowded in your body cavity. As your uterus expands in size, your internal organs get pushed back and upward, which puts pressure on your diaphragm and lungs. This means that you will increasingly feel shortness of breath. Keep this in mind as you run; you may notice that your breaths are shallower and a little bit harder to take. If you pick up the intensity, make sure to breathe as deeply as possible to avoid hyperventilation. Another fun part of your organs shifting is the wonderful moment when you can suddenly hear the gurgling of your intestines…right below your breasts. I recall this happening at around 25 weeks for me, and it was one of the strangest sensations I had felt during pregnancy. Fun fact: your internal organs don't necessarily *ever* return 100% back to their pre-pregnancy orientation!

Breasts

Boob changes. Notorious, in their own right, especially for those of us who never filled anything greater than a B-cup until pregnancy. To some, the newfound "fullness" is a welcome change. During her first pregnancy a runner friend of mine once said: "It's like the rest of puberty just happened!" Sometimes they grow gradually, other times it happens overnight. Literally, overnight. That was my big boob arrival. I shuffled into the bathroom in the morning, still groggy, and screamed when I looked in the mirror. Bras that fit the day before did not fit that day. This might have been the weirdest part of my pregnancy.

Needless to say, when this voluminous arrival happens to you, new running bras are in order. Some women like to layer two bras, with one or both of them being low-support (no underwire, minimal cup structure). Others will opt for one high-support bra fitting iron clad around the girls. It totally depends on your personal comfort and bra size, though remember to account for the fact that they will most likely still grow, especially postpartum. If you plan on breastfeeding and want to be able to breastfeed in running attire, look for bras with straps that latch on the front and are easily undone for nursing. Moving Comfort is the most popular company for these types of bras, though others are jumping on board as well (see Chapter 11 on breastfeeding and running for more details on bras.)

In the second and third trimesters, you may also notice some preliminary lactation, a sign that your mammary glands are in good working order and ready to nourish your little one. A key hormone called prolactin is to thank for this new bodily function. Expression of this early milk could happen at a random time, or when you are feeling somewhat "stimulated", shall we say. You'll notice a small amount of colostrum leak from the nipple. Colostrum is the body's first round of nutrition for baby, an incredibly rich blend of fats and sugar that serves to be a first meal when baby hasn't quite figured out how to nurse yet, but needs what calories he or she does consume to go a long way. It is yellowish in color, so don't be worried when your "milk" isn't what you expected!

Head

On top of everything else (literally, it's your head), it is common to experience headaches and dizziness during any and all stages of pregnancy. Be mindful of this while running. When you factor in all the other changes in your body, especially shortness of breath, a short "easy" run that used to be a piece of cake may suddenly render you a bit light-headed.

Recommended guidelines

Different doctors may vary in the precise recommendations about how hard you physically exert yourself during pregnancy, but in general, they will likely employ a fairly common-sense approach to "not overdoing it" and take your fitness, history, and health into strong consideration. The old adage, as seen in the ACOG (American Congress on Obstetricians & Gynecologists) guidelines from 1985-1994, was to "keep your heart rate lower than 140 bpm, your duration of exercise less than 15 minutes, and your core temperature below 38 degrees Celsius."[9]

Seriously? Only 15 minutes?

This recommendation changed for obvious reasons, and the use of heart rate as a metric for safety was also questioned. During pregnancy, your blood volume begins to steadily increase, and vasodilation of blood vessels fluctuates frequently in the first two trimesters, hence why shortness of breath and fatigue are common side effects of pregnancy. Because of these changes, the level of effort perceived at a given heart rate is in constant flux.[10]

Taking these factors into account, a more intuitive method has been found to be more useful in tracking how hard someone is working: The Borg Rating of Perceived Exertion (RPE) scale. (Figure 3). The scale ranges from 6-20, which may seem like an odd range, but conveniently,

---

[9] The problems with this old method was nicely summarized by this Australian doctor/runner on her blog: www.askdoctornat.com

[10] A great resource on pregnancy physiology for fit vs sedentary mothers: www.ideafit.com

multiplying a rating by 10 gives one's approximate heart rate at that given intensity. The scale works as follows:

6	No exertion whatsoever	HR = 60
7	Extremely light	
8		
9	Very light	
10		
11	Light	
12		
13	Somewhat hard	HR = 130
14		
15	Hard	
16		
17	Very hard	
18		
19	Extremely hard	
20	Maximum exertion	HR = 200

Figure 3- The Borg Rating of Perceived Exertion (RPE)

Per the Borg scale, pregnant women are advised to not exceed around 12-14 RPE. The heart rate (HR) values associated with the RPE values are convenient, but not necessarily accurate. A 1992 study in the British Journal of Sports Medicine compared HR and RPE values against each other and found that they did not correlate very well, recommending that RPE not be used as the *only* means of measuring intensity during pregnancy. Someone who is concerned about their intensity during exercise may benefit from *both* the use of a heart rate monitor and keeping tabs on their perceived exertion, but HR values will likely be inaccurate in the first two trimesters.

Generally speaking, though, if you have a healthy and uncomplicated pregnancy, and consistent dialogue with your doctor, you shouldn't require that much precision in measuring your efforts.

Here is what the ACOG has to say now:

"Recreational and competitive athletes with uncomplicated pregnancies can remain active during pregnancy and should modify their usual exercise

routines as medically indicated. The information on strenuous exercise is scarce; however, women who engage in such activities require close medical supervision.

Previously inactive women and those with medical or obstetric complications should be evaluated before recommendations for physical activity during pregnancy are made. Exercise during pregnancy may provide additional health benefits to women with gestational diabetes.

A physically active woman with a history of or risk for preterm labor or fetal growth restriction should be advised to reduce her activity in the second and third trimesters."[11]

In a nutshell, the following recommendations are agreed upon by most doctors and other running mamas alike:

> Listen to your body. Stop if something hurts.
>
> Stay hydrated! Keep water handy throughout the day, as well as during your run.
>
> Avoid running in high heat and humidity. *Stay inside* if it is above 90°F out there.
>
> Run in the early morning or late evening, to keep the sun off of you.
>
> Wear light, absorbent clothing. We runners love that stuff anyways.
>
> Try to run on even, steady terrain. You are more injury prone (more on why in Chapter 6) and don't want to risk falling.
>
> Take ample time to stretch post-run.

---

[11] The ACOG has significant resources on this subject: www.acog.org

Racing During Pregnancy

If all is going well with your pregnancy, including your running, you may decide to enter a race. It is a wonderful way to sustain your passion for competition! Many women do successfully race at various stages of pregnancy and across most distances, from Alysia Montano's 800m to Amy Kiel finishing the Boston Marathon, both over eight months pregnant.

Remember, always, that your pregnancy and your body may not be ready for their feats of prenatal athleticism. And that does not make you any less of a runner. Be inspired by their accomplishments, but do not attempt to mimic them.

Some things to consider, should you decide to race during your pregnancy:

Know your long-term goals. It is not uncommon to see heavily pregnant women running in local 5Ks and 10Ks, and it gets progressively rarer with distance. While there are several examples of mamas running full marathons and delivering healthy babies a few weeks later, make sure that you really evaluate your goals before deciding to do so. Can you train to complete a half or full marathon during your pregnancy? What do you want to get out of the experience? Did you get injured easily pre-pregnancy? How would this race fit into your long-term goals for yourself? Know the answers to these questions.

Don't try to PR! Even if you are in the early stages of your pregnancy, now is not the time to try for a major PR. While you won't necessarily cause yourself or your baby problems by training at high-intensity and racing at full-effort (that is, if you had already been training at this level pre-pregnancy), you might be setting yourself up for stress and frustration that you simply don't want or need during pregnancy. Save the PR for after baby. You WILL get there.

Take temperature into consideration. One of the biggest recommendations regarding exercise during pregnancy is staying hydrated and keeping your body from overheating. If you live someplace especially hot or if it's summertime, you may need to be carrying more water on your training runs. Do the same for a race in the same conditions, even if pre-pregnancy you wouldn't have dreamed of carrying a water bottle for a 5K.

Race with a buddy. If you're trying to maximize your intensity given your pregnancy, it could be helpful to run with a training buddy to help you keep your safe pace. If you're typically the type that just can't hold back and chat with friends during a race, maybe consider this a new training opportunity. Race with a friend or family member, and try to just enjoy the visit and the accomplishment!

Consult your doctor first! Discuss your goals and make sure your doctor agrees that they you and baby are healthy enough to race. Chances are, if you've been successfully training thus far, they will gladly give you the "go-ahead" to take to the start line.

Chapter 6
Your Pregnant Running Body: Beyond the Basics

Now that we've covered the basic wisdom on running during pregnancy, it's time to dig a little deeper on some of these points and discuss some lesser-known details. This chapter may come in particularly handy as a form of "troubleshooting", for lack of a better word, if you are experiencing pain or trouble during pregnancy. It is meant to give you some background on possible issues that can arise but is by no means a substitute for medical advice. We runners tend to be frequent culprits in crimes of self-diagnosis.

If you are experiencing ANY pain or are worried about how you feel, *talk to your doctor!*

Holy hormones, Batman

When we think about hormones and pregnancy, the first thing that comes to mind is typically the roller-coaster of emotions that many women experience. The ups, the downs, the sideways. Things that never used to elicit emotions in you are suddenly turning you into a basket case that you don't remotely recognize (those ASPCA commercials on TV? Don't even...). Of course, everyone goes through a different version of this. The role of hormones in your pregnancy and your running, though, is far deeper and more complex than just piloting your emotional state.

Hormones are the ultimate masterminds of your body. The conductors of your emotional symphony. The wielders of your immunity arsenal. The architects of your sacred womb. The great and powerful Oz. All of that, and more.

You might be well acquainted with the four major hormones involved in regulating your cycle: estrogen, progesterone, luteinizing hormone (LH) and follicle stimulating hormone (FSH). Surges in these hormones during your cycle have interesting and often conflicting effects on your running, as we will explore more of in Part III.

Even though your cycle is on hiatus, there are still significant hormonal changes going on. Let's take a closer look at the three major hormones that have the potential to impact your running.

Estrogen

As far as pregnancy is concerned, this hormone is the biggie. Estrogen is produced in the ovaries and steadily increases as pregnancy progresses, peaking in the third trimester. It is guiding the uterus's growth and aiding in baby's development. Although it is also responsible for symptoms like nausea and increased appetite, estrogen actually can have a positive impact on exercise. It acts on the hypothalamus to decrease body temperature, which comes in handy as you try to keep from overheating during exercise. Increased levels of estrogen also means improved bone density. All in all, estrogen is not a bad companion with respect to your running.

Progesterone

It might be helpful to think of estrogen and progesterone as "good cop / bad cop". Not to say that progesterone is bad; it plays a critical role in relaxing the uterine muscle tissue as it grows and expands, hence keeping you from going into labor too early. It works along with a couple of other key hormones to prevent your immune system from targeting the baby as a foreign invader. These are obviously good things! They do, however, have some side effects that can negatively impact exercise. Progesterone has the opposite effect on your hypothalamus as estrogen does, causing your body temperature to rise instead of fall. In its quest to keep the uterine muscles placid, progesterone relaxes *all* smooth muscle tissue, as well as blood vessel tissue. This is the reason why your blood pressure tends to drop during pregnancy, causing shortness of breath. Relaxed muscles in your digestive system can also mean heartburn, gas, constipation, and other discomforts. When in peak concentration, which is reached towards the end of the first trimester, progesterone can also stimulate ventilation, causing you to feel winded. When running suddenly gets more difficult than you feel it should, you can thank progesterone.

Relaxin
This is the ultimate double-edged sword of pregnancy hormones, and possibly the most influential on your running. Relaxin, as its name implies, is responsible for relaxing joints and ligaments in your pelvic region to prepare for the great expansion and push during labor. Like progesterone, though, it does not act *only* on the specific ligaments necessary for this job. It acts on everything, and its concentration in your system during pregnancy is about <u>ten times</u> its normal amount. At first glance, loose and relaxed ligaments may not sound like such a bad thing. Runners like to stretch, right? But remember that ligaments connect muscle and bone. When a muscle is contracted and pulls on the bone, you want those ligaments tight and strong for a secure connection and fast response. Loose ligaments mean micro-tears and strains in the muscle and subsequent scar tissue buildup when muscles are heavily exerted. In other words, you are much more susceptible to injury both during pregnancy and during many months postpartum, especially if you are breastfeeding.

As much as you may have the go-ahead from your doctor to continue in whatever level of training you had attained pre-pregnancy, and even if your physical fitness may outwardly seem intact, be aware that your hormone levels are making *big* changes that can impact your training performance and likelihood of injury.

Hips don't lie
In Chapter 5 we discussed "the waddle" and the impacts it can have on your sense of balance and the width of your stride. Pregnant women waddle when their pelvic alignment has changed to accommodate the forward shift in center of gravity. By taking a closer look at why and how the pelvis changes alignment, we also see that your muscles and tendons have to significantly adjust during the different phases of running gait.

Remember good ol' relaxin? That hormone exists primarily for this specific task: loosening the *symphysis pubis joint*. The pelvic bones on each side move apart, leaving a loose gap at the joint location (see Figure 4). This is the cause of "pelvic girdle pain" experienced by many women. This widening of the pelvis literally makes your hips feel a little wider and also causes your femurs to tilt slightly inward, making a subtle "V" shape. This change in femur alignment can have effects on your knees, ankles, and feet, as we will discuss in the next section of this chapter.

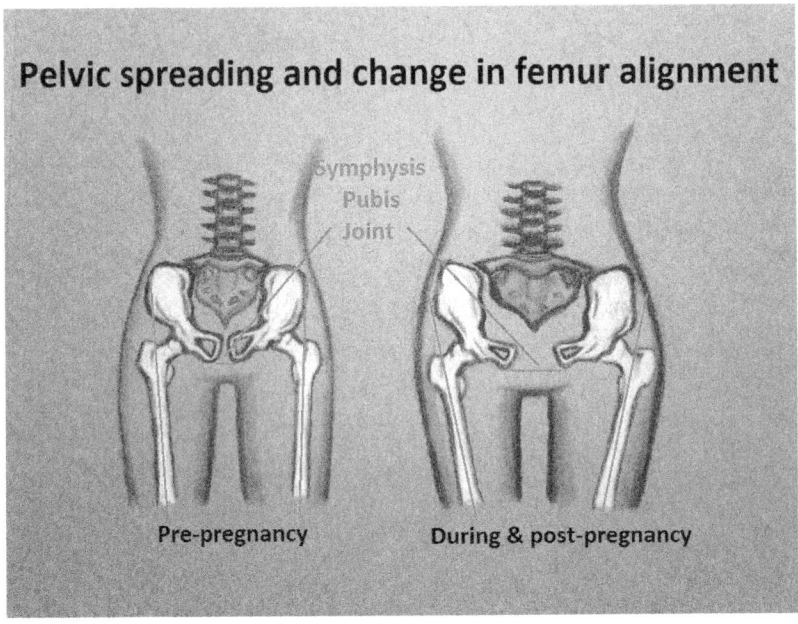

Figure 4- *The spreading of the pelvis during pregnancy*

One of the most potentially troublesome impacts of pelvic spreading is incurred by the hip and gluteal muscles. Picture in your mind: a suspension bridge, like the Golden Gate in San Francisco. The roadways are held up by suspender cables, which are attached to main cables, which are held up by the towers. The tension of all the cables depends upon the rigidity of the towers. If one or both of the towers were to tilt forward or backward, it would put a greater strain on one side of the main cables and relax the other side. The strained cables would likely break from the tension, and the relaxed cables would loosen to where they drop the roadway. Definitely bad news.

Regarding your running stride, your pelvis is like the bridge towers and your muscles and tendons are like the cables (albeit, the consequences of disaster in this analogy are disproportionate.) When your pelvis tilts forward, as we briefly discussed in Chapter 5 and as the symphysis pubis joint widens, your hip muscles are changing their orientation with respect to your femur, which is also changing to best support your weight. All of these adjustments in orientation mean some gluteal and hip muscles loosen slightly and others tighten slightly (see Figure 5).

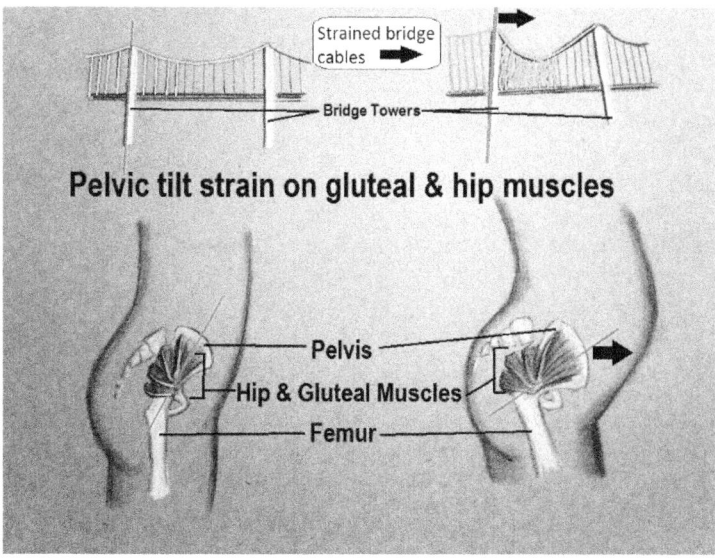

Figure 5- *A bridge analogy for the strain pelvic tilting places on hip & gluteal muscles*

This may not *seem* like a problem; after all, muscles are supposed to loosen and tighten as we contract and relax them, right? If a slight change in pelvic orientation really causes overstretching, how do gymnasts even exist?

Your muscles can certainly stretch and bend to move you through the ranges of motion necessary for running, sprinting, dancing, gymnastics, etc. But those are brief, rapid contractions, and only to the extent that your muscles have been conditioned to stretch (we can't all do the splits!) A subtle change in a muscle's tension while in its relaxed state, even if it is unnoticeable, can lead to micro-tearing and scar-tissue buildup when that muscles is then repeatedly contracted, and strained beyond its capacity with too much frequency. Over time, your muscles will certainly adjust to new lengths, just as they do if you practice yoga consistently over many months or years. These changes happen relatively fast during pregnancy, combined with relaxin running amok in your bloodstream, loosening the tendons that hold your muscles to your bones, hips, and gluteal muscles.

Your three gluteal muscles – gluteus maximus, gluteus medius, and gluteus minimus – usually don't feel the brunt of this change quite as much as your "deep six" hip muscles, also known as your *lateral rotator muscles:*

Piriformis

Gemellus superior

Gemellus inferior

Obturator internus

Obturator externus

Quadratus femoris

See these muscles in Figure 6.

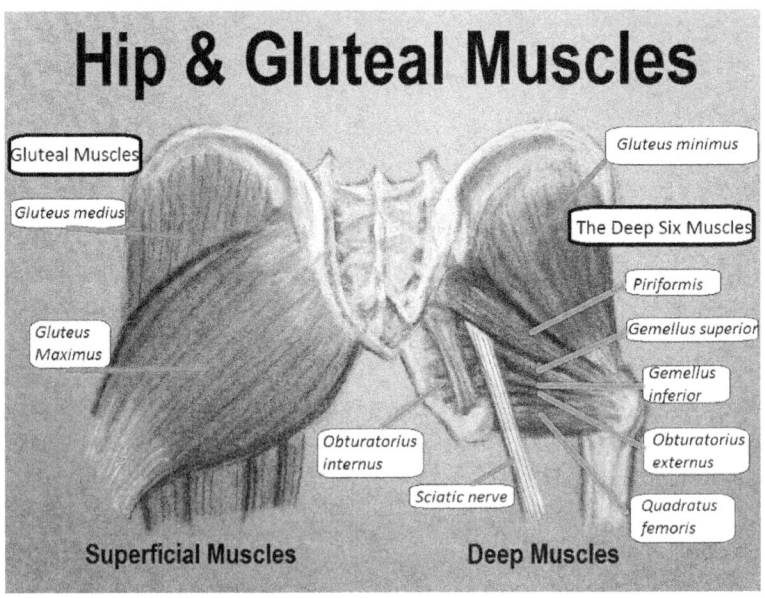

Figure 6 - *These muscles are at the crux of your running ability.*

These muscles serve to help rotate your femur within the hip joint, like a ball-and-socket. They are smaller and more intricate than the three gluteal muscles, thus more sensitive to changes in your pelvic framework. You may know them already if you have ever experienced *sciatic nerve pain*, as the sciatic nerve runs under the piriformis and across the top of the other five.

Sciatic nerve pain may be one symptom of possible strain in the deep six muscles. Scar tissue buildup around the strained muscles can pinch the nerve and cause pain along the entirety of it, all the way down the back of your leg and to your calf. This makes it challenging to diagnose the actual source of the problem, or pinpoint which of the many hip muscles is affected. Such injuries usually heal when the dreaded "r" word is applied: rest. But, hey, you're pregnant! Rest is important anyway.

The good news is that there are several types of medical professionals who specialize in these types of soft-tissue injuries, especially as they apply to running and sports in general. We will go over some of these techniques and approaches in Chapter 14.

No waddle?

Two days before I gave birth to my son, I was in my classroom obsessively cleaning my laboratory equipment (how scientists experience the "nesting" urge). I distinctly remember one of my students dropping by and saying "Mrs. Mikell, you're not even waddling yet! You're probably not going to have the baby for a while." I never did waddle during my pregnancy, and some friends, students, family, and total strangers commented on how lucky I was. Maybe because they assumed it meant that my figure wasn't drastically affected by my pregnancy. Our culture unfortunately tends to really glorify this idea of resistance to bodily changes brought on by pregnancy, which we will discuss in Part III. At the time, I simply thought "well, okay, cool. No waddle."

Not waddling came with some consequences.

In the last chapter and at the beginning of this chapter, we mentioned that "the waddle" is a result of two things: 1) your pelvis widening as the symphysis pubis joint loosens, and 2) your pelvis tilting forward as your center of gravity changes (see Figure 2 and Figure 5). Who knew that having 15-30 pounds of extra weight extending directly outward from your belly requires some adjustment in load-bearing?

In a way, the waddle is evidence that your frame has adjusted to best support the change in the amount and distribution of weight.

Women who, like myself, do not noticeably waddle may not be experiencing the same degree of pelvic shifting to accommodate the growing belly. It could simply be a difference in how much weight they are gaining and where it is being distributed; the pelvis of someone with a smaller belly doesn't necessarily need to shift much compared to the pelvis of someone with a larger belly. Though it could mean that the strain of the growing belly is compensated for elsewhere in the body.

Without the waddle, hence without significant pelvic shifting, lower back muscles may be working harder to stabilize your weight as your move. As we mentioned in Chapter 5, this can result in lower back muscle strains and a higher risk of disk herniation.

Despite how it might sound, not experiencing the waddle isn't *all* bad news. Following childbirth, your hips will return to their pre-pregnancy orientation more quickly. Your running stride won't change as much, and are less likely to experience some of the lower-body strains and issues (mentioned below) that are a result of pelvic spreading. Enjoy those perks! Just be aware that your body could be compensating for the change in center of gravity elsewhere.

Pronation and arch collapse

You've likely noticed some foot swelling, which is the biggest reason why shoes just don't fit the way they used to. But there is another culprit for your sudden need to upgrade your running shoes.

Many women experience arch collapse over the course of their pregnancy and in the months following. This will cause your feet to measure slightly longer. Imagine an inch worm in the crunched-up phase of its movement versus the extended, flattened phase. When your arch is strong and well-supported, it is like the crunched up worm. When collapsed, it is like the extended worm. How much this can change depends on how high your arches were to begin with. If you were already flat footed, there's nothing to collapse.

Arch collapse during pregnancy has three primary causes:

1. Weight gain

2. Over-pronation

3. Hormones

Since weight gain is an inevitable and obvious part of pregnancy, it makes sense that it is a contributing cause of many physiological changes. As you gain, more pressure is put on your arches, and the harder they have to work to maintain rigidity. This can be a source of foot discomfort, from dull aches to fleeting but sharp pains across the bottom of the feet. Time for a massage!

Then there are the anatomical forces affecting your arches. The changes in your pelvic width, as we already discussed, can cause your femurs to tilt inward, making a slight "V" shape. This can be cause for knee pain, and make you somewhat "knock-kneed." Your knees are experiencing more weight than they are used to, yes, but also from a slightly different angle. It may not be noticeable to you, but your knees know what's going on. This strain translates down the legs to your tibias, which place an increased force on your talus and navicular bones, as seen in Figure 7. This can cause your feet to over-pronate, which is commonly associated with collapsed arches.

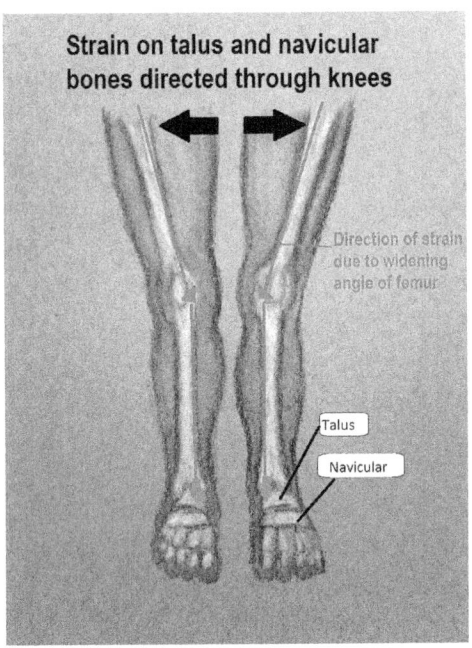

Figure 7 - How the change in hip spreading affects your legs, ankles, and feet.

Then there are the hormonal influences on foot changes.

As we have already discussed, an always-critical yet occasionally problematic hormone serving active duty in your pregnant body is relaxin. It's hard at work making sure that your tendons are flexible enough to endure significant stretching during childbirth. Because relaxin is a systemic hormone (prevalent in your bloodstream), it affects all tendons, not just the ones involved in birth. The tendons that uphold and support your arch can loosen during your pregnancy, also contributing to arch collapse.

Pronation

Pronation *refers to the inward "tilt" of the ankles when you take a step. A neutral pronator's ankles tilt inward slightly or not at all; an over-pronator's ankles tilt inward excessively; a supinator's ankles tilt outward. There are many structural and functional factors that affect pronation, including how a runner strikes the ground. If they land on their heels, they are more likely to experience pronation than if they land on their mid-foot* *or forefoot. For this reason, we can't really equate having low arches or flat feet to being an over-pronator, but the arches can affect pronation and vice versa. With little or no arch, the talus and navicular bones drop downward more extensively when weight is placed on them during the contact phase of one's stride, hence over-pronating.*

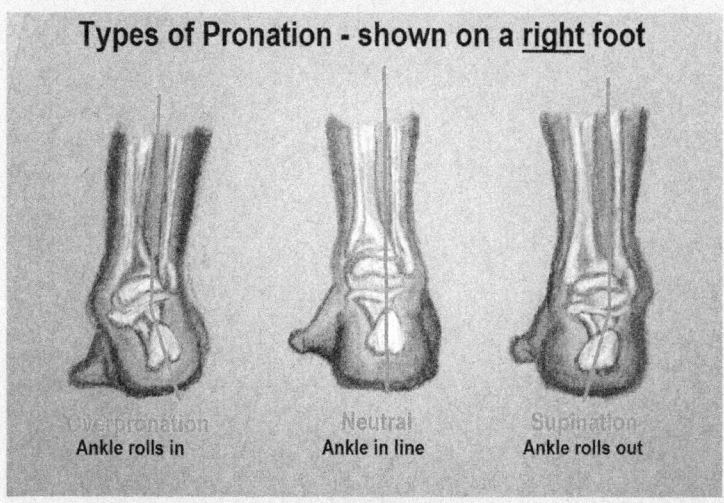

There is some debate in the running community on the subject of pronation and how it affects running efficiency and injury susceptibility. Most running shoe companies make motion control and stability shoes to provide support for over-pronators by attempting to stop the excessive inward roll of the foot. But many exercise physiologists suggest that since over-pronation is the result of many physical and kinetic forces in an individual's build, stopping its motion can cause more harm elsewhere in the body. Some runners change the extent to which they pronate over time as they improve their stride efficiency and running economy, perhaps as they begin striking the ground further forward on their feet and reducing the opportunity for their feet to "roll in". This aspect of running physiology is a fascinating and complex topic to investigate!

Mind the gap

Your abdominal muscles do some serious spreading during pregnancy to accommodate that beautiful belly. Both during pregnancy and after delivery, this can mean a condition known as *diastasis recti*, a gap between your abdominal muscles (Figure 8).[12] When the muscles themselves are spread apart, all that connects them is a thin tissue layer. Damage to this tissue can occur when the abdominal region is put under any significant strain, as might occur with heavy lifting (hence the general advisement against it). Even swimming and some yoga poses can worsen diastasis recti.

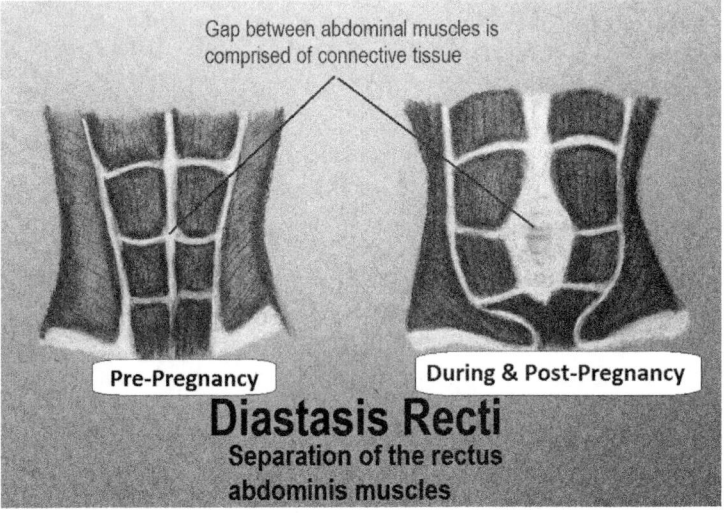

Figure *8 – Spreading of abdominal muscles.*

Abdominal spreading is not going to cause you any significant problems or pose any issues for your baby. But it is an issue of poor stability of your upper body; the weakened abdominal region means your body takes strain elsewhere trying to compensate, making lower back pain more likely. So is a weak pelvic floor, interestingly enough, which can mean a higher risk of incontinence and leakage.

Not all women experience this; stronger core muscles pre-pregnancy reduce the likelihood, so adding a little bit of ab work early on can help prevent spreading.

How to recognize it if you have it:

    1. Lay flat on your back and place two fingers just above your belly button.

---

[12] WebMD gives some great "do's" and "don'ts" of diastasis recti.

2. Inhale and relax your abdomen.

3. Exhale while bringing your shoulders slightly off of the floor.

4. If you feel a space in between your abdominal muscles, you've got diastasis recti!

Some core strengthening can be done to "bridge the gap" and prevent further abdominal spreading from occurring though it is important not to over-do it. Crunches and sit-ups, for example, actually *worsen* the issue as those muscle contractions pull the connective tissue farther apart.

Exercises to avoid if you are concerned about diastasis recti:

Any types of crunches

Planks

Oblique twists / Russian twists

Reverse leg lifts

V-ups / Pilates 100s

The types of exercises you *do* want to do are those that engage the core muscles in stabilizing your posture. Basically, any exercises that don't involve bending your belly inward.

Exercises to help prevent or treat diastasis recti:

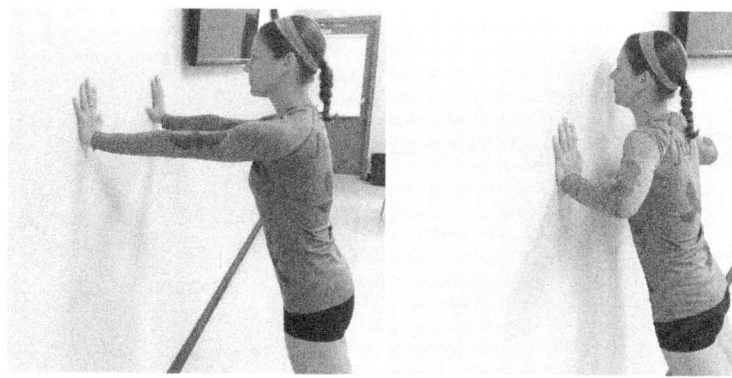

Figure 9 - Upright push-ups: improve your overall core strength and posture without putting too much strain on your abdominals. Like regular push-ups, only vertical.

Figure *10* - *Squats against the wall. You want your back to be straight and focus on "being tall", without feeling too much strain in your mid to lower abdominals (underneath hand). This is great for strengthening your hamstrings and hips, too.*

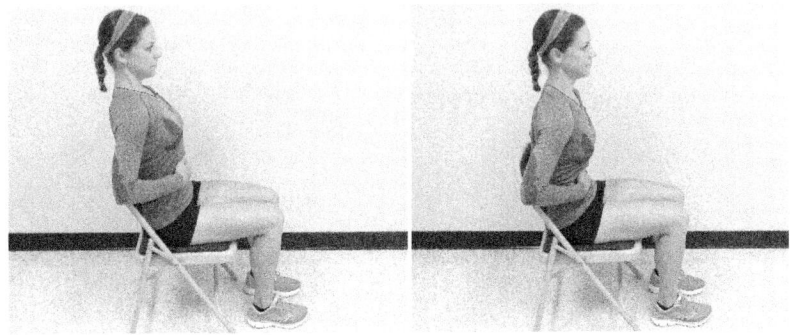

Figure *11* - *Seated squeeze & core contraction. Place your hand on your mid-abdominals. Start with your back upright against the back of the chair (left). Inhale. When you exhale, gently contract your abdominals beneath your hand (right). Think of pressing your* belly button to your spine.

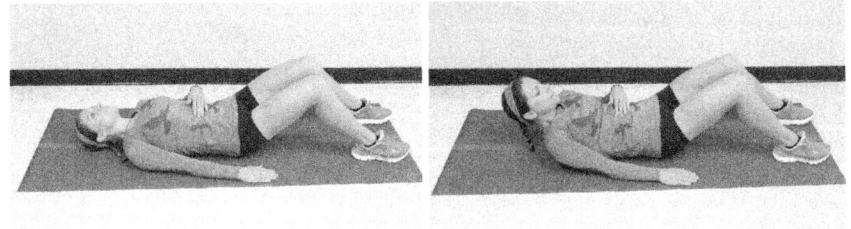

Figure *12* - *Laying head lift. Place your hand on your abdominals. Keep your back flat on the mat and your head relaxed (left). Gently lift your head from the mat, without doing a full crunch (right). You want to feel a slight squeeze in your abdominals but not fully engage* them. *If you have* diastasis recti, you should feel a gap in your abdominals just *between your fingers (where my hand is* placed).

Generally speaking, your abdominals will reconnect over the course of several months postpartum. For runners, though, it is all the more important to retain a stable core, not just to prevent back pain, poor posture, and a weak pelvic floor, but also to prevent hip injuries that you are already at a higher risk of incurring. More on this issue in Chapter 14.

Change of heart

One of the biggest changes experienced during pregnancy occurs beneath the surface: your cardiovascular system. The structural changes to your body can only occur if the building and supply crew does some overtime. Good news: these changes can actually have some long-term positive effects on athletes!

In his book, Exercising Through Your Pregnancy, reproductive biology researcher Dr. James Clapp referenced five major changes that occur in your cardiovascular system during pregnancy:[13]

>   1. *Increased blood volume*
>
>   2. *Increased skin blood flow response (hence "the glow" of pregnancy)*
>
>   3. *Increased heart chamber size*
>
>   4. *Increased blood volume pumped with each beat*
>
>   5. *Increased oxygen delivery to all tissues*

For obvious reasons, some of these changes are very much welcomed by runners. Take, for example, blood volume. Over the course of pregnancy, a woman's blood volume can increase by 40-50%! There are two primary reasons for this increase:

>   1. *To optimize the exchange of nutrients between mother and baby. Higher blood volume means increased osmotic pressure across the placental tissues.*

---

[13] Clapp makes a very compelling and well-written case for continuing exercise during pregnancy, particularly for the positive effects during delivery and the health of the baby thereafter.

2. *To prepare for possible blood loss during delivery. That's right, your body makes you backup blood!*

These changes in your blood volume have implications for your perceived effort during exercise. If you've trained with a heart-rate monitor before, you likely know what your resting heart rate is. That is, you think you know. During pregnancy, your resting heart rate changes due to this increase in blood volume combined with the loosening of vessel tissue (which causes a slight drop in blood pressure, despite the higher volume). It can increase by as much as 20 beats per minute from your pre-pregnancy resting rate. Like everything else, this effect varies from woman to woman and is another reason why the Borg Rating of Perceived Exertion may be a better indicator of your running intensity than going off of heart rate.

Three of the other changes – increased heart size, blood volume pumped per beat, and oxygen delivery – are adaptations that many endurance runners are constantly trying to achieve through training. You get them all in a few months as a little pregnancy bonus! In Part III, we will discuss how these adaptations affect your running postpartum, as well.

Chapter 7
Nutrition & Pregnancy

Food and pregnancy. Probably the most controversial of all pregnancy-related topics. Spend ten minutes on Google and you discover that apparently everything is bad for you and baby. I wish I had restricted myself from internet access completely during the first trimester and avoided a good deal of senseless worry. But ignore the internet completely and you will still receive endless unsolicited advice from family, friends, and total strangers about what you can and cannot eat.

My advice? Take it with a grain of salt.

(See what I did there?)

Nothing will cause you more stress during pregnancy than fearing that the chocolate cake you just indulged in has too much caffeine and might cause you to miscarry.

Here's a quick summary of the recommendations by the American Pregnancy Association (APA):

1. Avoid foods that might be contaminated with the bacteria, *Listeria* or *Salmonella*, which can cross into the placenta and infect baby (not all bacteria necessarily do). These include:

   Raw or undercooked meats, of any kind

   Raw egg

   Deli meats (unless you heat them to kill any possible bacteria, which also kills the point of eating a cold turkey sandwich if you ask me)

   Unpasteurized cheese, milk, or other dairy

   Smoked seafood

2. Avoid caffeine during the first trimester, after which consume in limited amounts (less than 200mg / day, which is around 2 cups of regular coffee).

3. In addition to bacteria concerns, limit fish consumption due to environmental toxins (mercury, for example).

4. No alcohol. This one is an obvious no-brainer.

5. Wash all fruits and veggies thoroughly before eating.

Some of these guidelines could still be contested on the basis of how pregnant women eat in other cultures; many Japanese mothers give birth to perfectly healthy babies having eaten sushi through their whole pregnancy, and in many European cultures, pregnant women may consume small amounts of wine or beer. Nutrition science is a very tenuous field of research, especially when it comes to pregnancy; not many expecting mothers are willing to be test subjects. There are no guarantees. There are just trends and risk factors that correlate with possible problems or complications.

Bottom line: know the risks, make the food choices that are right for you, and relax. You're a competitive runner, so a healthy diet is likely already a big part of your life and making minor changes for pregnancy is not going to rock your boat too much.

Eating for two?

We have all seen many portrayals of pregnant women in movies and television, and generally they are about the same: a physically-uncomfortable but "glowing" mom-to-be either experiencing mood swings, weird food cravings, or extreme nausea. She is most likely eating a very large meal or asking her helpless-looking husband to go to the store and buy pickles and ice cream for the cranky and emotional Pregzilla on the couch.

The many stereotyping problems with these scenarios notwithstanding, there is a perception that women can eat considerably more when pregnant, and that eating for two means, literally, eating twice the calories they did pre-pregnancy. When I was pregnant, I can't count the number of times a fellow female said to me, "you can eat whatever you want now and it's OK because you're pregnant!" They were quite disappointed to hear that I was not, in fact, eating everything in sight. Following their mistaken philosophy, many women gain an excessive amount of weight during pregnancy and do not return to their pre-baby weight in the following months or years. Remember, your baby is significantly smaller than you and floating weightlessly in liquid! He or she just needs enough calories to grow and metabolize, which is not nearly as much as what an adult needs.

To maintain a healthy pregnancy and provide enough food for your growing baby, according to the APA, you only need to consume an <u>extra 300 calories</u> during the second and third trimesters. That's an extra bowl of oatmeal with nuts and fruit. And whether you are pregnant or not, quality always matters. Your health and the health of your baby will, of course, be greatly improved by choosing fresh, quality sources of calories over empty, sugary calories. But that doesn't mean that an infrequent brownie sundae with hot fudge isn't warranted.

Good grief, you're making a human! You deserve occasional indulgences.

Training fuel

Now we need to factor in your running.

If you're burning more calories, you will need to consume more calories to make up for the deficit, in addition to the additional 300 you need anyway. Generally speaking, we burn about 100 calories per mile, whether we walk or run that mile, with some fluctuations based on intensity, hills, sweat, and other variables. So let's say you're in the second trimester and you go run three miles. That day, you should aim to consume 600 calories more than you normally would under pre-pregnancy and non-running conditions.

The best way to ensure that you do this is to eat a moderate snack right after your running. In any case, the "window" of one hour post workout is the best time to consume a protein and carbohydrate snack, pregnant or not, for optimum recovery from your run. But it isn't necessary to get too technical about it. If you are well "in-tune" with your body's hunger cues, you may opt to simply follow them during pregnancy and training.

In general, simply following your hunger is OK. Nutrients are passed from your bloodstream to baby's in the placenta, and your hunger is generally a good indicator of how much is needed at any given time. Your metabolism will take what it needs for baby, first, and leave you the rest.

Consider how pregnant women have successfully given birth to very healthy babies on much lower-calorie and lower-nutrient diets than most of us are accustomed to. You probably don't need to calorie count or do any food measuring to ensure you are getting about 300 extra calories per day. Just make sure those are nutritious calories that give you a balanced spectrum of vitamins and minerals. Quality is just as important, if not more important, than quantity.

If you have concerns about getting enough food to your baby, discuss it with your doctor at your next visit. He or she will know from your weight gain and from measurements of the baby taken during ultrasounds that your little nugget is growing at a healthy rate.

There is one thing I need to make clear at this point in the chapter: avoiding the cultural tendency to overeat does *not* mean you should fear gaining weight, even and especially body fat. You will and you must.

Worth the weight

It is obvious that a growing baby will mean weight gain. Not just the baby, but the placenta, amniotic sac, amniotic fluid, and other supporting tissues add to the growing weight of your belly. But the weight itself is not the whole picture of a healthy pregnancy. The composition of that body weight matters.

Women *must* sustain a certain amount of body fat for a healthy pregnancy.

How much body fat they gain depends entirely on the woman; her body fat percentage pre-pregnancy, her frame and size, and genetics all play big roles in weight gain during pregnancy. Some women have a healthy amount of body fat pre-pregnancy and only put on twenty or thirty pounds during. Some women put on sixty pounds during pregnancy, mostly body fat, and lose it all in the months following. Some women appear to put on very little body fat and are "all belly" during their pregnancies. Unfortunately, our culture tends to glorify the latter to the extent that some women worry about gaining body fat and attempt to diet during pregnancy.

Pregnancy is NOT THE TIME for weight loss!

There are exceptions to this in some cases: women who are very overweight or obese pre-pregnancy and need to lose some weight for their health and the health of the baby. Some women who suffer from *Hyperemesis Gravidarum,* a condition of very severe morning sickness, may lose weight in the first or even second trimesters, despite the growing baby. Such cases may require bedrest or hospitalization, even supplemental hydration, but usually result in perfectly healthy babies.

If you are not experiencing either of those situations, you should expect to gain some body fat during your pregnancy, especially around your thighs and hips. This storage of energy provides lasting backup calories to the developing baby and also maintains proper hormone function. Do not fear the fat! It is there to help you create and sustain a healthy baby.

Mighty Mama: Lisa Valentine

Age: 54

Home: St Petersburg, FL

Profession / Run life: Cross country & track coach, sub-2:50 marathoner, sub-18:30 5K, frequent local master's champion.

Children: Five grown kids: Sophia (29), Clayton (23), Bradley (20), Steven (19) and Rachel (17), and one new granddaughter, Vivienne!

Photo by Chris Lauber

In 1998, I ran my first Marathon ever (trained by Coach Joe Burgasser). I was happy to have run 2:59 and felt I could do better. The better news was *that I was pregnant soon after and had my beautiful daughter Rachel, nine months later. I tried so hard to run. No go. At 5'3" and 106lbs, it was uncomfortable, more like impossible. I decided to stick with the stair master and step aerobics the entire time I was pregnant. In September I gave birth to Rachel (my youngest) at age 37 and decided to train for the Boston Marathon the following year. That gave me a bit over 6 months to get ready.*

Because I kept my fitness up the transition was easy, as was the weight loss (yes, I ate and ate while pregnant, gained over 40lbs and pretty much lost it all quickly.) Went to Boston and ran a solid 2:50. Staying fit while pregnant was key. If you can't run find other ways to work out. It will keep you strong and feeling good. Diabetes runs in my family...my mother passed away from it at age 48. I'm 54 now and a Grandmother. I will run until the day I can't. Until then, my dream is to pass the torch to the next generation while continuing to be a participant. I coach the Cross Country Team at Canterbury School of Florida, and my hope for them is to run forever.

Being a running mama of 5 has been a wonderful experience. Having a team that knows your kids, priceless. My kids all have their own activities and we nurture that. Coach Joe Burgasser and his wife Wendy are the center of our running family. Having an awesome husband (Dwight) by my side has been such a blessing. The weekends are for the kids and our family. We like it like that.

Chapter 8
Keeping Perspective

With all of the structural and hormonal changes we described in Chapter 6, it is to be expected that your feelings about running, pregnancy, and life, in general, will go through some fluctuations. Creating ways of keeping perspective and cherishing this incredible time of pregnancy is so important for you, your family, and your baby. These ways may or may not involve your running, but they will most likely involve those closest to you.

Patient partner

Ever have a strong memory of a conversation or even just a few words exchanged that appears meaningless on the surface, but what transpired in your own head during that dialogue made a powerful impression?

One morning during my third trimester, my husband and I had just awakened from a rough night of me tossing back and forth in discomfort. I was an instant grump. He asked me how I slept and I snapped back at him, "Are you kidding me? Did *you* actually get sleep?" He put his hands up in surrender and smiled. "Nope, I was just trying to be funny." He left the room before I could issue any more accusations; smart man. What I remember so strongly is how I was mad at him either way, whether he did get sleep or not. If he did, *how dare he get sleep while I can't!* If he didn't, *what's his problem? He doesn't have a human tumbling around inside his abdomen!* From that point onward, I made a conscious effort to be more empathetic towards him. The fact that I had the lion's share of physical changes to bring our child into the world did not mean that he wasn't also experiencing stress, poor sleep, and anxiety, or that he shouldn't be feeling those things. He is the other half of the parental unit, after all.

If you have a wonderful person like this in your life, make it a priority to be empathetic toward them, and ask about their feelings, worries, excitement, all of it. The voyage of pregnancy belongs to both of you, and it is easy to get caught up in the notion that you are the lone traveler. Remember that when baby arrives, you *both* will be adjusting to a new schedule, new responsibilities, and less sleep. While you are protecting your running or other fitness activities in your schedule, make sure that your spouse can do the same. Sharing is caring. Consider taking a Babymoon so that you can bond and rally your collective strength and love in preparation of your newborn.

Advice, everywhere

There is one interesting part of the pregnancy contract that you probably don't remember signing when you decided to become a sacred vessel of life: you are now an instant magnet for unsolicited advice. From everyone. Everyone. Everywhere. All the time.

One important thing to always remember: such advice is *well intentioned*. Nobody wishes harm on you or your baby (if they do, you need to re-evaluate your social circle).

Repeat this mantra in your head: *they mean well*.

You'll need it, as there <u>will</u> be times when you have to fight the urge to punch, slap, or otherwise maul the next person that says you shouldn't be drinking that coffee, don't put your arms above your head, you *must* hire a doula, you need to paint the nursery pink if it's a girl, or basically everything else that can be said. Some advice will certainly be good advice, but that doesn't actually matter when it is unsolicited and you've been hearing it nonstop for three trimesters. It could be the best idea in the world and you'll still grind the crap out of your teeth.

As a runner, you may be gifted with an extra bonus of opinions, especially from members of the older generations. Family, friends, and co-workers will likely know you're a dedicated runner and trust that whatever you and your doctor have discussed is the right thing. Its total strangers that may get on your last nerve the most while you are on a run, maybe shouting that you shouldn't be running, yell profanity at you, or even shout a prayer directed towards your baby (a runner friend of mine heard this once).

This might not be the most satisfying tip, but the best way to deal with unsolicited advice is a simple smile and nod. If that's not your style, try a diversion tactic, like asking how so-and-so is doing and change the conversation. With strangers, just ignore them, and maybe invest in some quality headphones to use on your run. Whatever you feel like doing, as long as it doesn't cause you additional stress or make you feel that you are doing something wrong. If they make a comment that causes you to second-guess something you are doing, or not doing, and it starts keeping you up at night, talk about it with your doctor. If people close to you or anyone you interact with regularly are being a bit too consistently incessant in their unwanted advising, it might be a good idea to have a conversation about it and politely ask them to stop. Most likely, they will respect your wishes.

Remember, *they mean well.*

Incredible body

As we talked about in Chapter 7, weight gain and body changes are a necessary part of pregnancy. This sounds like a "duh!" sort of statement, and yet many women become saddened or distressed when it happens to them. When we start showing, we are excited. The growing baby becomes visibly evident and most of us carry that badge with pride. When baby weight starts showing elsewhere on our bodies, however, we tend to resent it. Yet that weight is just as important as the growing bump.

That weight represents your body's programmed ability to sustain the growing person inside of you. The body fat that you put on is nature's brilliant failsafe. When you think of it this way, your body's changes are actually freaking incredible.

Just like Nadia Comanici's perfect 10 on the parallel bars was incredible.

Just like Paula Radcliffe's marathon world record was incredible.

Just like the moment you PR'd in your favorite race distance was incredible.

There are so, *so* many different ways that our bodies do 'incredible' and yours is now commencing. Embrace this! When you look in the mirror as your body grows and changes, make it a point to smile at yourself. Relish in the change. Be proud of your body's versatility.

Your body will get back to being an incredible running machine before you know it.

Mighty Mama: Christa Benton Stephens

Age: 32

Home: St Petersburg, FL

Profession: Music teacher

Run life: Florida State XC champion for three years while in high school, holds 5K times under 17 minutes, sub-3 hour marathoner. Her husband, Lee, is also an all-star distance runner.

Children: Son, Adriel, born in June 2013.

What about your pregnancy surprised you, in terms of how your training was affected?

After the initial surprise of finding out I was pregnant wore off, mostly I was surprised that I really didn't feel much different than normal most of *the time. I still had some fatigue and loss of appetite and food aversions throughout the first trimester, but besides that I felt pretty good and had no problems training throughout the pregnancy. I loved being pregnant even more than I loved running. Once I heard from my Ob/Gyn that continuing with my running routine with care not to push myself too hard would not harm my baby, I was at ease and ready to run with my baby. I guess I was expecting to feel greatly different being pregnant and not able to run or to hear my doctors discouraging me from running during pregnancy, but I was pleasantly surprised to be able to comfortably enjoy running and training throughout my pregnancy and feel good doing it.*

How long after delivery did it take for your "training groove" to return?

I started back pretty quickly and probably didn't take the full recommended number of weeks off. I had an uncomplicated delivery and felt pretty good. I remember that I started back walking the day after my son was born through the hospital halls (after suggestion from a nurse). I would push my newborn son in his wheeled hospital baby crib cart and we would go all up and down the hall ways a couple times before getting discharged. When we got home I gradually progressed to walking several loops around the neighborhood each day. After a several weeks of just walking, I gradually added in some jogging. I felt good jogging but was careful not to overdo it by going too far or too fast. After about a month, my jogging turned back into running. When Adriel was about 6 weeks old, I won my first race as a new mama. It was a beach 5K. I was careful not to outdo myself in the race but still maintained a solid effort. It was just a little after this time- maybe when my son was 7-8 weeks old that I started to feel like I had gotten back into my "training groove".

What part of your training was modified the most, both pre and postpartum?

I was very fortunate to be able to run regularly throughout my pregnancy. I still smile when I look at a picture of my baby boy bump breaking the finish line tape of a 5K I won when I was about 6 months pregnant, and I laugh when I remember how I jogged several miles on my son's due date hoping that it might help get some baby action started. Still, I would say that my training was greatly altered mostly by reducing the quantity of miles and the intensity of the runs. As soon as I found out we were expecting, I made sure to not push my intensity level above the point where I felt like I was running too fast to not be able to get a full breath of air. I figured as long as I had enough breath in my lungs to be able to talk or sing a little bit then I figured my baby would have enough air and blood flow to be comfortable too. I never had a heart rate monitor, but I think that would have been a good idea to wear if I had owned one. Anytime I did an interval workout or fartlek I would keep the intervals at 6 minutes or less of faster pace and then have some recovery jogging in-between sets. I also decided that I would not race any distance longer than 5K throughout my pregnancy. I have heard of several pregnant mamas racing longer distances, but I decided that on my own knowing how competitive I get and felt the most comfortable with that. Once I was 7 months pregnant, I decided that I would stop racing and doing speed workouts altogether just to avoid the temptation to go too fast during the 3rd trimester. During this time, my husband talked me into cutting my mileage back more and by the 8th month of pregnancy I began taking my husband with me on all my "runs" which were mostly just jogs at this point. (I figured it would be nice to have my husband with me if I started to go into labor on a run.) My baby boy was overdue and came a week late. Around his due date, my doctor joked that they would ordinarily recommend that I get out and jog a couple miles, but he said in my case it probably wouldn't help my baby to come any faster. I even ran the day before my son was born, but it was pretty slow.

As for postpartum training, I just remember taking things easy and doing a very gradual return to running after some walking and jogging first.

Did you battle with any lingering injuries in the months/years following pregnancy?

Yes, though I can't say that I had any major injuries, I have struggled on and off with minor aches or injuries mostly in my hips and hamstrings. There are good days and bad days, but it tends to flare up if I overdo it on speed work, particularly on tracks, or if I try to run too much mileage without adequate rest. Another thing that helps me to keep injury away is to routinely stretch, do proper warmup, and strength training.

Do you breastfeed? If so, how has that impacted your training?

Yes, I breastfed for a little over a year. It was very natural and efficient and some beautiful and precious bonding time with my boy. I probably would have breastfed for longer, but my son began showing signs that he was getting ready for weaning just after he turned a year old. He would gradually nurse for shorter periods and would drop feedings all on his own. This made the weaning process easier for me as I felt reluctant to try to wean quickly. Breastfeeding came pretty easily for the 2 of us, and by the time we were home from the hospital my son was regularly nursing 8-9 times as day with about 2 night feedings. By one month old, my son was down to just one night time feeding. At 2 months old, my son was regularly sleeping through the night all by himself. When it came to training and breast feeding, I just made sure to nurse before running if possible because I always felt more comfortable running without full breast. If I couldn't nurse, then I would pump and have a bottle ready for him. I had an electric pump as well as a portal hand pump that was very helpful. After weaning at about 14 months we had lots of frozen breast milk over from pumping and my son had breast milk until he was over 18 months old.

Any specific tips on staying healthy / injury free that you recommend for competitive new mamas?

I would recommend every new mama do their best to ease back into their running routine gradually. Also it would be important to schedule time to work on strength training with weights. If an athlete mama is struggling with and recurring pain or muscle imbalance or weakness, I would recommend to look into physical therapy exercises to strengthen the weak area. I've never tried much of these next two suggestions, but I think yoga and deep tissue massages would be helpful too.

How did you cope with sleepless nights, time constraints, and work schedules in those early new baby months?

We had a very good scenario in that I am a school teacher and our son arrived just a few weeks after the end of the school year and we would be together all of summer vacation. School started up again when my son was just over 7 weeks old, but he started sleeping through the night about 7 hours straight once he turned 8 weeks old. We were also fortunate that my husband was willing and able to take time off work to be a stay-at-

home dad. Having one of us with him at all times was very helpful for our family. But we knew we could ask for help if we needed. My mother was able to form a very close bond with her grandson and was always ready to come over if we needed a break or wanted a run. We also had lots of support from all of our family. We were very fortunate and blessed to have all the help. My best advice for new mamas getting used to a new schedule would be to try sleeping when the baby sleeps and also ask for help from family and friends if you need it.

Has your relationship with competitive running changed since becoming a parent? If so, how?

Once I found out I was pregnant I immediately had a new purpose in mind when it came to running. Instead of training to be the fastest, I wanted to run to feel strong and help my baby have a healthy pregnancy and hopefully a smooth delivery. Once I had my son and started running again, I thought I would quickly return to the competitive athlete that I had been for so long... In many ways I am still that same competitive athlete trying to get a fast time on the run, but in one very important way I am forever changed. Now I am a mother too. This fills my heart with such joy and I can't imagine things any other way.

PART III – YOU RECOVERING

"In giving birth to our babies, we may find that we give birth to new possibilities within ourselves." – Myla and Jon Kabat-Zinn

Chapter 9
Postpartum Running: The Basics

CONGRATULATIONS, MAMA!

Welcome to parenthood, or if this is not your first baby, welcome to *more* parenthood. You have just endured an incredible feat of the human experience and are in store for many adventures ahead. Running is likely not as strong in your mind as it usually is, which is perfectly natural. But when you are ready to get back in the saddle, this chapter is here for you!

When to run again

Most doctors recommend that you take at least six weeks of rest after giving birth, more if you had a cesarean section. This corresponds with the first postpartum check-up when they can evaluate how you are holding up. While most women tend to follow this, some have been successful at returning sooner simply by following how their bodies feel and taking it very, very slowly. These women likely engaged in fairly moderate training up until their delivery. In all likelihood, you will welcome the downtime and appreciate the recovery process. But if you are considering resuming your running routine earlier than the standard six weeks, here are some key things to look out for:

> *Any abdominal pain – stop if you feel it*
>
> *Stitches from an episiotomy, if you had one (these should be long gone before you consider running!)*
>
> *Incontinence or other pelvic floor issues (see next section)*
>
> *Knee and other joint pain*

The most important thing about deciding when to return to running is to keep perspective. You don't need to return at the same time as someone else did. There is no upcoming race that is worth you injuring yourself or not properly recovering from pregnancy, and starting a running program before your body is ready is a guaranteed ticket to problems. Don't rush!

Birthing ground-zero

The region of your body most impacted by giving birth is, quite obviously, your pelvic floor region. As you are now well aware of if you had a vaginal delivery, a significant amount of blood and mucous is passed in the first day or so after giving birth. A surprising amount. I remember the nurse telling me to keep an eye out for clots, and not to worry as long as they are smaller than a grapefruit. *A grapefruit!* Hearing that, I was terrified to try to see what was going on down there. The reality, though, is pretty incredible.

The tissue surrounding your cervix and vaginal opening begin the healing process as soon as your baby and the placenta have made it out. Your uterus will drop in size from watermelon to pear within a matter of days! Your pelvic floor muscles also begin to heal, but because they have had to undergo a significant stretch, they need some time to regain tension and control.

During this time, many women struggle with incontinence. Running can exacerbate this problem due to both frequent leg movement and the force of your organs pounding down on the pelvic floor. It is not something that everyone experiences necessarily. I have started to humorously speculate that runners may actually experience it less than non-runners for one simple reason: we are *very* accustomed to holding in #1 and #2 on long runs, so we really should have pelvic floor muscles of steel.

In any case, the pelvic floor muscles may take a few weeks to regain their strength, and this is one big consideration when doctors advise the six-week rest period.

C-Section recovery

The recovery process is definitely different for those who have a cesarean section than it is for those who have vaginal deliveries. In general, as I mentioned before, it usually requires a longer recovery time. Though you do not need to worry about your pelvic floor muscles, you will likely still pass blood clots for several weeks postpartum. Most women report that they spend much of the first couple of weeks in bed, as their abdominal regions can be too sore to do much else.

The ACOG advises *total rest* of six weeks postpartum to allow the uterine tissue and incision region to fully heal, followed by some easy walking, which can actually help with blood flow and reduce clotting. During this time, there is a risk of incision scar infection, and likely some scar tissue buildup in the uterine muscle itself. Just like with your running muscles, scar tissue buildup can cause some pain and discomfort when those muscles contract.

Allowing your body to fully heal is your top priority right now. Jumping back into running too quickly can interrupt your uterine healing process, which can mean problems down the road if you intend to have another baby one day. Some women return to running sooner than others, and there is certainly a wide range of possible outcomes. It is highly recommended that you get the OK from your doctor before you start running again.

Foot folly & bra business

As we discussed in Chapter 5, foot swelling and arch collapse can cause you to go up a shoe size...or two. For some women, their new shoe size is a permanent change. Others return to their pre-baby shoe size as they recover from pregnancy as their arches re-strengthen.

If you have been running through your pregnancy, you already have good-fitting running shoes, and chances are your feet won't get *bigger* postpartum. If you have not laced up the trainers during pregnancy, the first time you do so after baby is born could be frustrating. If you decide to purchase new running shoes, make sure they are truly your *new size*, not what you think you should be wearing. The worst thing you can do is run poorly-fitted shoes when you jump back into training. Get that extra half-size up, or wide size. Believe me, it's worth it. By the time you have worn those shoes out, you might even be back to your old size.

If your feet haven't grown in size, rest assured that other things have. With your newly-enlarged set of breasts, it's time to invest in some new running bras! Some women go up two or even three cup sizes while others merely fill out their existing cup sizes just a tad more. It is possible, too, that in the earlier months of breastfeeding, your breasts will be at their largest, and then gradually go down in size when baby begins solid foods or starts weaning altogether. In addition, breasts may be *significantly* larger when full than they are when empty, making it challenging to size a running bra.

Some general tips for choosing new running bras:

1. Size flexibility – some have adjustable straps.

2. Front closure (zipper) or Velcro straps– makes breasts most accessible for nursing.

3. Removable padding in the cup - can give a little extra support, and can be removed to give a looser feel in necessary. Also can hold nursing pads!

4. No underwire, *unless you really need that extra support* – can put too much pressure on milk ducts, which can cause plugged ducts and mastitis. You're better off doubling-up your bras to keep the pressure evenly distributed.

5. Do a bounce test – jump around, a lot.

These types of running bras can be a bit pricier than you may be used to spending on running apparel. But they are well worth it if you think you will nurse while wearing the bra or are significantly larger-breasted post-baby.

Some of the more popular brands that make nursing-friendly running bras are:

Moving Comfort

Maidenform

Enell

La Leche League

Many of the more mainstream running gear companies (New Balance or Brooks, for example) may make a bra model that has the front closure and works just fine for nursing.

If you don't foresee yourself needing to nurse while in your running attire, and you are comfortable wearing your pre-pregnancy running bras, by all means continue to do so. Some mamas double-up on their regular running bras for support, or simply put a running bra on over their regular nursing bra. Ace bandages can make great extra bra support.

One critical suggestion: do not leave your running bras on for longer than necessary, especially if you start to feel engorged after a long run. Running bras put more pressure on your breasts than your regular nursing bras and wearing them for too long, which can lead to a plugged milk duct (more on that in Chapter 11).

Jogging strollers

One of the most fun new elements of being a running mommy is the prospect of strapping junior in a jogging stroller and taking him along on a run. It can be a wonderful experience to share your enjoyment of running and the great outdoors with your little one!

For most joggers, your little one needs to be able to sit upright on their own in order to sit safely and comfortably in the jogger, which is usually around 4-6 months old, at the earliest. Most joggers are compatible with car seats, which click into an attachment point on top of the stroller with baby facing you. Most of these stroller systems, however, advise only walking with this configuration on the basis that the bouncing from running is too intense for baby.

There is a plethora of joggers out there to choose from and it can be overwhelming trying to decide on a good stroller. Generally speaking, there are some key characteristics that we all want in a stroller:

> *Reasonably light weight*
>
> *Maneuverable and easy to handle – especially folding and getting in and out of your car*
>
> *Good shade for baby*
>
> *Safe and comfortable for baby!*

Most strollers you come across meet these requirements. Then, for runners, there are a couple other details to choose from:

Fixed or swivel front wheel

Hand-brake or no hand-brake

Fixed wheel strollers (like mine, shown in the following pictures) are generally considered to be more stable at faster speeds than a swivel wheel, and usually have hand brakes which gives you a little added bit of control for a quick stop. Swivel wheel strollers, though, have the option of being locked into place while running yet also the benefit of superior maneuverability when used otherwise. If the difference in stability at high speeds matters to you, then a fixed wheel is a good choice though some seriously fast running can still be accomplished in a swivel wheel.[14]

Consider if you will be doing most of your training without baby, early in the morning while baby is still sleeping and family are at home, or whatever schedule is working best for you. Regardless of how often you use your jogger, running with baby is a great option to have, especially when there are opportunities to run with other mamas or do a family run-outing.

It is important to note that pushing a jogger is definitely challenging and causes you to modify your running form. Putting too much weight down on the hand bar, slouching (Figure 9.1) or running with your arms locked (Figure 9.2) can all have negative impacts on how your hips drive you forward, increasing risk of injury. Some runners run with one hand on the hand bar, others with two. One hand is just fine, as long as you frequently switch! You want to keep your back straight and not lean on your stroller, arms slightly bent to allow some give with the stroller's movements (Figure 9.3).

---

[14] The record holder for running a marathon with a jogging stroller, Michael Wardian, used a BOB Revolution, which is a swivel wheel, to run 2:42:21.

Figure 9.1 - **Bad form**. *Slouching can have detrimental effects on your back, and pretty much everywhere else.*

*Figure 9.2 - **Bad form**. Locking your arms can cause tension and strain in your lower back, and over-reaching in your stride can pull too much on your hip muscles.*

Figure 13 - Good form, running with one hand (left) and with both hands (right) on the hand bar. Back straight, foot landing directly under hips, elbows slightly bent.

Joining a tribe

Group fitness activities for mothers and babies are abounding these days, at least in most towns and cities. They range from running groups complete with jogging strollers to "mommy and me" style aerobics or yoga. This could be a fun way to start your running routine up again once you have recovered from delivery.

Depending on what type of group you join, they may also be serious runners and have some running-specific wisdom to share as well. You might feel much better running with other running moms than flying completely solo.

It's also a chance to get some "mommy networking" in. Other local moms usually have all the goods on baby consignment stores, the best playgrounds, good babysitters, day cares, and everything else you can imagine. They are your best resource, hands down, on everything baby-related in your community.

This is a facet of new parenthood that I personally wish I had become more involved in; it is somewhat symbolic of a more innate, tribal tradition of a community taking care of its children together. That is pretty darn wonderful.

Chapter 10
Postpartum Running: Beyond the Basics

In addition to the basics we covered in the previous chapter regarding your running body postpartum, you can generally expect much of what was also covered in Chapter 6, when we went "beyond the basics" of running during pregnancy. Aside from suddenly being 15-20 pounds lighter than you were before, much of the physiological conditions of pregnancy are retained for several weeks, or months, or even longer if you are breastfeeding. In addition, your body has some obvious healing to do, as we discussed in Chapter 9.

This is definitely a time to listen carefully to your body's signals that it might not be ready to start running again. When you first start to test out your running parts again, it may come back very naturally with minimum discomfort, or it may be an unpleasant struggle for a while. Either way, know that your body is still behaving, in some ways, as if it were pregnant.

Hormone shift

As you can imagine, your hormones have endured perhaps the most significant event in your body's history, as far as they are concerned. Some hormones that have gradually increased in your system during pregnancy undergo a sudden drop postpartum while other hormones quickly climb in concentration. Imagine them as giving each other high-fives as one leaves the playing field and another enters.

Using our handy sports analogy, we can examine the following groups of hormones postpartum.

These hormones that are "tagged out" as soon as baby is born:

> **Progesterone**
>
> **Estrogen** – though it will gradually increase later on to sustain prolactin production
>
> **Relaxin** – though still remains higher than pre-pregnancy

The "ringer" hormones that kick-in during labor and delivery but then drop back down:

Corticotropin-Releasing Hormone (CRH) – *keeps your body from rejecting the baby as a "foreign" invader and helps trigger labor.*

Adrendocorticotropic Hormone (ACTH) – *released as a result of CRH, this stress response hormone mitigates the release of cortisol...*

Cortisol – *stress management hormone. Apparently your body thinks that giving birth is stressful.*

Adrenaline – *so much for managing your stress! Get PUMPED! You're giving birth!*

Endorphins – *nature's way of making you think you freaking love giving birth so that maybe you'll do it again one day.*

The following hormones are "tagged in" during or after labor and delivery:

Oxytocin – *this hormone actually gradually increases during the third trimester and triggers labor by stimulating uterine contractions. It will stay in the game postpartum, but does spike during labor and delivery. Oxytocin is also a "bonding hormone" which helps to release intense feelings of love and closeness between mom and baby after delivery. A pretty cool way for nature to make sure that a mother definitely wants to care for that tiny human that just caused her so much pain! Oxytocin also kicks into gear when baby suckles on the breast, and in turn can cause the contractions that bring your uterus back down to normal size.*

Prolactin – *this hormone stimulates milk production in mom's mammary glands, and also has a direct relationship with the stress response system; prolactin is often elevated in conjunction with cortisol as a stress response, even when no lactation is necessary or occurring. Exercise, since it is a stress on your body's internal environment, actually stimulates prolactin levels as well. It also suppresses the follicle stimulating hormone (FSH) which is responsible for ovulation and fertility. With FSH kept low, nursing mothers usually don't regain their fertility until they wean their* babies (*but not always! You can still ovulate and get pregnant while nursing!*) Prolactin also has a significant impact on mom's sex drive, which we will discuss further in Chapter 12.

Some mothers have reported that their hormones were more out of control during the first few postpartum months than they ever were during pregnancy. This can be especially true for hormones that affect mood, as both oxytocin and prolactin can do. In Chapter 12, we will talk about the emotional changes that come with this challenging time.

In terms of running, changes in estrogen and progesterone tend to have the biggest impact on your general perception of effort. As we talked about in Chapter 6, estrogen has the effect of decreasing your body temperature, where progesterone increases it and causes your blood pressure to drop. For these reasons, you tend to feel your "best" when estrogen is dominant in your system and have the highest perceived difficulty when progesterone is dominant.

The core of the matter

Also during Chapter 6, we discussed the issue of diastasis recti and how to prevent it. If this does happen to you, know that your ab muscles *do* eventually re-join on their own without much conscious intervention. But because they have undergone some stretching during pregnancy, they have weakened and may have an impact on your posture, which, when you run, can impact your back, which can impact your hips, and so forth. It is important to be aware that these kinds of weaknesses in your core muscles can have negative consequences on your running form and stability. That having been said, commencing a crunches boot camp right after giving birth can actually *prevent* healing.

In order to repair and strengthen your abs, you need to do frequent, steady moves that reinforce the joining of the muscles yet not exacerbate their separation. Check back to Chapter 6 for demonstrations of good core-strengthening moves that help prevent and heal diastasis recti.

Still hip

In Chapter 6 we also closely examined what happens to your hips, glutes, and lower back during pregnancy and the implications they have on your running. These implications still hold true postpartum for several months.

Your hips take time to re-join at the symphysis pubis joint and your musculature is still adapted to move your body under pregnancy conditions: more weight and a more forward center of gravity. These changes mean that your running form is, once again, going through changes.

While the outcome of change is not necessarily bad, the process of change keeps you injury prone. As the hormone relaxin is decreasing in your body, tendons and ligaments are re-tightening. Overall, this is a good thing for your running strength, but can come with some minor aches and pains in the process, particularly in your pubic region as your pelvis re-connects.

Hip muscles are the biggest culprits of postpartum running injuries, especially the "deep six" muscles that we identified in Chapter 6. Remember that your hips have changed orientation and are in the process of changing again, putting new strains on all of the muscles attached to them. Add in the hormonal changes, the re-tightening of ligaments, and possibly weakened running form, and this dynamic is all the more sensitive. All aches and pains should be taken note of, but especially the hip and glute region.

Some tips for preventing hip injuries postpartum:

1. Start your runs with form drills! These will reinforce good form and get you warmed-up with dynamic movement.

2. Run slow and easy at first.

3. Be conscientious about your posture and form, especially during harder runs and workouts, even if it requires you to slow down somewhat.

4. Stretch your hips and hamstrings gently, but consistently, after running.

5. See a sports doctor ASAP if there is consistent pain!

Bone blues

Some new mothers, runners or otherwise, have experienced sharp pains in their hip socket in the weeks and months following pregnancy. This can be a condition known as *transient osteoporosis*. In an x-ray of the hip, the femoral head, which is the top part of the femur that sits like a ball in the hip socket, shows degradation and weakness in the latter part of pregnancy and postpartum period.[15]

How exactly this happens isn't entirely understood; one hypothesis is it may have to do with the constriction of blood flow in that region due to a big heavy belly to support, thus less calcium delivered to the lower body, and the femur is ground down with each step.

Meanwhile, on the other end of the femur, another similar condition can follow from transient osteoporosis: *transient bone marrow edema*. This is indicated by knee pain and swelling; those are obviously symptoms of a variety of knee conditions, but this one pertains particularly to the latter stages of pregnancy and the postpartum period. The lower end of the femur wears down the knee cartilage and undergoes "bruising", both from the increased pressure exerted on it during pregnancy.[16] The good news is that both conditions usually resolve themselves over the course of several months, hence the "transient" nature of the condition.

The danger for runners, though, is exacerbating the problem by putting too much stress on these sensitive joints in the lower body during that weakened time, causing stress fractures. This is another good reason to ensure good calcium intake during and after pregnancy, which we all should be doing regardless of pregnancy!

Blood boost

As previously mentioned, pregnancy causes an increase in blood volume of up to 50% by the end of the third trimester. This ensures that there is enough blood to "push" nutrients across the placenta and that oxygen transport can keep up with a growing baby. What is also particularly awesome to us runners is that *stroke volume*, the amount of blood

---

[15] Recommended treatments for transient osteoporosis can be found here: http://orthoinfo.aaos.org/

[16] A very interesting comparison on two female athletes postpartum and their injury woes: one woman who ran through her pregnancy and the other who spent most of her pregnancy on bedrest, both wound up with knee injuries.

pumped with each contraction also increases by 25%. More blood moving means more oxygen moving means a higher VO2 max! Sounds like a pretty awesome new-baby gift from Mother Nature.

Unfortunately, these wonderful adaptations don't stick around forever. In the first year postpartum, however, your blood volume, cardiac output, and stroke volume still remain somewhat elevated before dropping back down to pre-baby values. Many elite runners have scored themselves PRs within the first year of pregnancy, posing speculation that a "postpartum advantage" may be created by this increase in VO2 max, though there is little evidence on this subject and not nearly enough data linking, specifically, the increased blood volume and the improved performance.[17]

In any case, your cardiovascular system is, in many ways, strengthened by your pregnancy. Think of it as constant strength training, carrying around that extra weight, plus the blood volume changes to nourish your baby. Even if you engaged in *no* exercise for your whole pregnancy, your cardiovascular system would still be strengthening itself and your blood volume would increase. It's like secret training! Of course, you would lose overall *fitness* from not exercising, but there are long-term adaptations taking place that will improve your athletic ability down the road when you return to training and regain that fitness.

The biggest adaptation is your heart's capacity to pump blood. Even when your blood volume returns to normal, your heart's efficiency at moving blood will have improved over your pre-pregnancy cardiovascular capacity. If you did train through pregnancy, you will come back to your pre-baby fitness more quickly. If you did not, you will still have a stronger heart to come back to.

Rest for the best
Of utmost importance during your first few postpartum weeks, make sure that you are getting enough rest. Believe me, I totally understand how tall of an order that is when you have an infant! Your body normally undergoes a great deal of repair at night while you sleep, and unless you are very lucky, baby is probably waking you up frequently. It might be time to implement naps into your daytime schedule. Pretty much

---

[17] *Competitor Magazine* did an excellent article on this subject in 2013.

everyone you know will recommend you "sleep while he/she sleeps" during maternity leave or however long you are home with baby for. Much easier said than done when there are so many other things you need, want, or otherwise feel compelled to do during the rare time that baby doesn't need your attention. But your bones, muscles, tendons, heart, and mind all require more rest than you may realize. Take heed! You'll be stronger tomorrow if you do.

Your recovery from pregnancy aside, this rest will benefit your running in very surprising ways. As you will read in Chapter 14, when I interview my sports doctor, most professionals who work with runners agree on the biggest reason behind a "postpartum advantage" that seems to occur in competitive female runners: *REST*. The downtime you get during pregnancy and postpartum allows your running-related body parts to rest and repair themselves, which they normally would not get if you were in the midst of your normal training cycle rather than pregnant.

Like most of us, maybe you have had some aches and pains that you had ignored for months, or years. Or maybe you were never injured, but weaknesses in your form and a lack of strength training gradually weakened your body without you realizing it. Whatever the case, the rest from your pregnancy and your immediate weeks postpartum will repair problems you may not even realize you had. We will get more into this in Chapter 14.

Mighty Mama: Stephanie Rothstein Bruce

Age: 31

Home: Flagstaff, AZ

Profession / Run Life: Elite runner for Oiselle and Hoka OneOne, coach for 'Running with the Bruces' and team member of Northern Arizona Elite, holds 2:29 marathon PR and 1:10 half-marathon PR.

Children: Riley, age 1. New Baby Bruce due in September 2015!

What about your pregnancy surprised you, in terms of how your training was affected?

My first pregnancy was very much planned and I was coming off of an injury so not training that much to begin with. I experienced horrible morning (all day sickness) for the first 15 weeks so running/working out were not a priority. Surviving on the couch was my MO. Once I got through the worst of my sickness I began running 20-35 miles a week and incorporated 1-2 light workouts a week. The first couple of runs I was surprised at how labored my breathing was and how high my heart rate was despite the effort being the same as my normal easy run. That continued until about 20 weeks and then I had this huge surge of energy in which I felt great training. Your body gets a crazy amount of extra blood flow in the 2nd trimester and this made running feel awesome. I was able to maintain training through about 32 weeks and then my pelvis got too uncomfortable so it was an easy sign to stop running. I approached training very light hearted my first pregnancy as the priority was to listen to my body, grow a healthy baby and have my body get used to being pregnant.

How long after delivery did it take for your "training groove" to return?

I had a fairly rough delivery so it took by body a full 6-8 weeks to feel "normal" again. Of course postpartum there is a new normal so I just did my best to accept the changes my body went through. Once I was able to start running (about 7 weeks postpartum) I took it very slow running 5-10 minute runs for a few weeks. Everything just felt different and out of place "down there" so I wasn't very comfortable. Add in the pain of swelling breasts from breastfeeding and strapping on a sports bra over those puppies and things were looking grim. It took me about 3 months to see glimpses of my old self training wise and then I began running times in workouts I'd never been able to before. The biggest surprise was how quickly my cardiovascular fitness came back even though my musculoskeletal system wasn't as prepared. There were also things that women don't talk about much that I experienced while running postpartum. I had many bathroom issues and feelings of heaviness in my lower pelvic area for many months postpartum. Most of it I'm sure had to do with having a 9lb baby who was born sunny side up. He did a number on my pelvic floor.

What part of your training was modified the most, both pre and postpartum?

The mileage and eventually the paces. I couldn't run as many miles as my normal training simply because I didn't have the energy to and wanted to ensure I wasn't taking anything away from the growing baby. I probably averaged about 50% of my normal mileage (80-90 miles per week). I was able to still run paces that were similar to when I'm training while not pregnant, up until 25 weeks or so. That's when I started to really slow down as my belly was growing and the pressure down below was increasing. Postpartum I approached training as if coming back from a major injury. Your body needs time to adapt to the stresses of running again so I built up very slowly and took it week by week.

Did you battle with any lingering injuries in the months/years following pregnancy?

My pelvis was the biggest issue that lingered for about 4-5 month postpartum. It was not in the right position due to the delivery and loss of my abs so I had to perform a ton of breathing exercises, glute activation, and ab bracing exercises for a few hours each day to correct the pelvis position. There was no fracture but the muscles around it were trying very hard to stabilize and just became fatigued.

Do you breastfeed? If so, how has that impacted your training?

I breastfed exclusively for 4 months and then my supply started to drop so we brought in formula until I eventually stopped around 5 months. It was an interesting adjustment to get used to in the beginning. I didn't realize how tired it made me until the day I stopped and got a huge burst of energy and thought "wow, nursing really zapped me." As far as the actual effects on training I just had to time my runs and workouts a lot around the baby's eating schedule. So the first feed in the morning, I'd breastfeed then head out the door for my run or workout knowing I had about 2-3 hours to get in my work before he needed to eat again. Luckily when we built up a surplus of milk in the freezer I had some leeway and my husband could give him a bottle and I just pumped when I got home. The other funny part about breastfeeding as an athlete is having your milk supply fill back up mid workout and leak through your sports bra on your cool-down. Something every female runner should experience!

Any specific tips on staying healthy / injury free that you recommend for competitive new mamas?

Strength training and preventative exercises are very important to me during pregnancy and I try to maintain them the entire duration except for those uncomfortable last 7-10 days. The main areas of the body I focus on are the glutes, hips and back. Working on your core is fairly ironic as you want that area to stretch during delivery so strengthening more only works against you. I like to focus on bird dogs, clams, and a routine of 5-6 glute activating exercises. I aim to perform these 5-6 times a week as long as I can. Granted there will be "pregnant" days where no amount of exercise will be performed and take these days when you need them! If you do these exercises during pregnancy you're more likely to continue them postpartum which is very important as you ease back into your training routine. Keep me in mind that while breastfeeding your ligaments are looser and more susceptible to injury so be sure to progress training gradually.

How did you cope with sleepless nights, time constraints, and work schedules in those early new baby months?

I wouldn't say there's any true "coping" with the sleepless nights but rather letting them run their course. It's a necessary part of the first few weeks while your baby needs to eat every 2-3 hours and if you're breastfeeding you're the only one who can bear that load. I took steps to ensure I napped during the day when the baby was napping and tried to cut down on my extracurricular activities around the house. Having a support system was crucial to my mentality and strength postpartum. First off being around my husband and teammates who are also professional runners has allowed me to live vicariously through them and helped keep my goals and dreams in perspective. So on those days where the sleeplessness really got to me I was available to keep the big picture at hand. I tried to utilize the time I was awake by checking items off my to-do list. You start to prioritize what's really important to get done and what can wait. Luckily my job as a professional runner allows me to be home 24 hours a day so my "work schedule" was flexible around mine and the baby's needs.

Has your relationship with competitive running changed since becoming a parent? If so, how?

It hasn't changed too much as far as my goals. The biggest change is probably that I have 2 jobs: one as a mom and one as a professional runner. My time management skills have improved as you learn to become much more efficient with your time once you have a little one around. My coach, Ben was hugely instrumental in helping me get back post baby as he met with me weekly to write my training and adapted it to my needs *based on how I was recovering, how the baby was sleeping, etc. My team of chiropractors and massage therapists worked with me through pregnancy and postpartum keeping me healthy and aware of my strengths and weaknesses. I haven't returned to my old self yet as I'm getting ready to have baby #2 soon but hope to get back to the competitive side of the sport once I recover from this second pregnancy.*

Chapter 11
The Nursing Runner

Deciding how you want to nourish your baby is a very personal and important choice. There are pros and cons to both breastfeeding and bottle feeding which depend exclusively on the specific lifestyle of each and every mom. No mom should feel pressured to adopt one method over another. I am focusing on how breastfeeding affects runners since there are physiological impacts that do not exist for runners who opt to formula-feed their babies, and are therefore not lactating; I am not advocating one choice over the other.

From a purely running standpoint, let's look at some pros and cons of breastfeeding while training:

Pros:

Helps you resume pre-baby body weight quickly

Retains consistent bonding time with baby during an otherwise busy schedule

Delays the return of your period, sometimes for the entire time that you breastfeed

Great reason to purchase larger-sized running bras

Cons:

Engorgement

Possible interference with training and racing to nurse baby

Relaxin hormone stays in your system, maintaining your injury-proneness

Mastitis is a real "you-know-what"

Demanding supply

During the first few weeks of nursing your little one, you will likely find yourself in awe of how effectively your body responds to baby's nutritional demands. The first few days of that rich, yellowish colostrum can be particularly befuddling; I remember wondering how such a small amount of the stuff could be so filling to my newborn! The more he suckled, the more my body gradually began to make, until my regular supply of milk "arrived". This period of time can also be stressful for a new mom, wondering when her supply will kick in and if it will be enough for baby. Some mothers struggle with producing enough milk and opt to supplement their breastmilk with formula. There are lots of ways to get baby the nutrition he or she needs, and it sometimes takes time to fall into a successful nursing routine.

What is really remarkable is how your body mechanically and hormonally responds to the frequency and quantity of baby's nutritional needs. Supply and demand really does apply. The more baby nurses, the more milk your body will produce. It may not happen right away, but over time, this is usually the case. Nursing moms have to consume enough calories to produce milk, which is usually about <u>500 extra calories</u> per day, give or take a little depending on how big baby is and how much he or she nurses. As baby grows, and consumes more milk, supply can temporarily drop somewhat until your mammary glands get the message and kick into a higher gear.

Understandably, some mothers are concerned that exercise can lower their milk supply through burning extra calories and water loss. Whether or not this happens is highly individual; some moms really struggle with supply just by running three miles a day, while others can train for ultramarathons and never see a drop in supply.

Let's consider some of the physiological characters in this play.

On one hand, we know that very high-performing female athletes can experience amenorrhea (no period) during their most intense training years. It is, therefore, clear that hormones are affected by intense exercise, and not a stretch to imagine that such affects could similarly cause changes in lactation.

On the other hand, as we have mentioned before, it does not make evolutionary sense that milk production could be easily impaired by a relatively small reduction in calorie intake, be that a result of restricting calories in one's diet or burning calories through exercise. Burning calories on even the most rigorous weekly mileage doesn't even come close to the calorie deficit many mothers have endured throughout human history, and our population is now over 7 billion.

Numerous studies have been conducted in the past couple of decades on the effect of exercise on breast milk. Specifically, they ask two primary questions:

1. *Does exercise affect the <u>volume</u> of milk produced?*

2. *Does exercise affect the <u>composition</u> of milk?*

Nearly all of the studies have shown that milk volume production is not affected by moderate exercise, and rarely affected by high-intensity exercise.[18] In fact, one study even showed a *positive* association between intense exercise and milk supply.[19] As far as composition is concerned, parameters such as hormone levels and macronutrient content (protein, fat, carbohydrate) have likewise been studied in exercising and non-exercising women; no difference in composition has been found.

While the biochemical components of lactation do not seem to significantly change with exercise, one biochemical component of exercise could potentially have an effect on the taste of breast milk.

Tastes like lactic acid?

As you're probably aware, lactic acid is that delightful waste product found in your bloodstream after your body has undergone anaerobic respiration (you're moving too fast for oxygen to be used) and broken-

---

[18] KellyMom.com is a wonderful resource for scientific publications on this topic, and just about any topic pertaining to motherhood.

[19] This 1990 study also analyzed some milk composition parameters in exercising vs. non-exercising mothers, finding that *"There was no difference between the groups in plasma hormones or milk energy, lipid, protein, or lactose content. Exercising subjects tended to have higher milk volume (839 vs 776 g/d) and energy output in milk (538 vs 494 kcal/d)."*

down muscle tissue in the process. The heavy, painfully-sore legs after running a 400m dash are closely associated with lactic acid.

Like many molecules that can pass from your bloodstream into your breastmilk, lactic acid has been measured to do the same. The intensity of exercise, though, does matter. You do not produce lactic acid at low to moderate levels of exertion when no muscle breakdown is occurring and your efforts are mostly aerobic (you're moving slowly enough for oxygen to be used). At high levels of intensity, in which your muscles are undergoing significant anaerobic respiration, some lactic acid does end up in breastmilk.

Does this harm baby? No, not at all. At worst, milk *could* taste slightly sour to baby immediately following exercise. After I gave birth to Jack, a fellow runner advised me to pump-and-dump after intense races, as her babies didn't like the taste of lactic acid. This is another highly-individualized issue.

Concerns about this issue were raised in a 1992 study published in *Pediatrics* when a group of babies fed breastmilk pre and post-exercise were far less accepting of the milk after exercise. The problem was how the milk was delivered in the study: babies were breast-fed before but bottle-fed after, so their change in acceptance could have easily been a preference for breastfeeding over bottle-feeding, not any change in the milk itself.[20]

Later studies that *did* control for the delivery of breastmilk found no difference in the babies' reaction to the milk. Again, this is a statistical find, so *some* individual babies out there might indeed notice an unpleasant taste in breastmilk following mom's intense workout. If that is the case for you and your baby, the good news is that lactic acid will clear from your milk progressively over the next hour or so.[21] In the same way

---

[20] An excellent example of why one should examine the methods of a study before fully accepting the validity of its results.

[21] This study compared non-exercising lactation to post-maximal exertion lactation. The concentration of lactic acid that can accumulate in milk is a direct function of how hard the mother exerts herself in exercise.

that a small concentration of alcohol consumed by a nursing mother infiltrates breastmilk, it will also clear from the milk in exactly the same way it clears from the bloodstream. So there is no need to "pump and dump"; any lactic acid that might be present in the milk will leave the milk on its own.

Plugged ducts & mastitis

There could come a time, or two, when "the girls" temporarily turn on you. The occurrence of plugged ducts and mastitis are fairly common, and can be mild in nature as well as knock you on your butt for days. Plugged ducts occur when an engorged milk duct becomes "clogged" with milk and globules of proteins. A part of your breast might feel hard and tender to the touch. Sometimes, if the plugged region is close to the nipple, you might observe a white dot where milk should be coming out during letdown, but is not.[22] Plugged ducts might be painful for a while until the clog passes though tenderness and a firm feeling might persist for a day or so.

Mastitis is what can happen when a plugged duct becomes infected. You experience all of the symptoms of a plugged duct *plus*:

Fever, chills, aches, like the flu

Red streaks or patches on the plugged region of the breast

Loss of energy

Headache

If you are experiencing these symptoms, call your doctor. Mastitis can often require antibiotics to treat. Your doctor will also give you advice on treating a plugged duct or full-blown mastitis at home. From my own experience, I have found that the following treatments work quite well for alleviating a plugged duct and for dealing with mastitis (which are also what you will see recommended if you do some digging on the web):

---

[22] For those soon-to-be new moms who have not yet experienced letdown, milk does not flow from one opening. There are multiple openings in each of your nipples. It's not a single, steady stream. It's a showerhead! This had me quite taken-aback the first time.

NURSE YOUR BABY AS OFTEN AS POSSIBLE on the affected breast. This might be somewhat painful, but it is the best way to unplug the plug. Don't worry about passing on the bacteria that have infected your milk to baby; it's a relatively small amount of bacteria and his/her stomach acid will take care of it.

Hot and/or cold compress on the affected breast. I have found alternating these to be particularly effective.

Rest. If you have mastitis, don't even think about going for a run. You probably won't have the energy to, anyway.

Drink lots of fluids.

These breast conditions do not affect everyone. Many women make it through breastfeeding just fine without either of them. But runners are particularly susceptible because we spend a substantial amount of time wearing tighter bras than usual. Constriction or excessive pressure on the breast is the biggest culprit behind plugged ducts. The early stages of weaning are also prime time for mastitis to strike, as well as when you are sick since general inflammation can contribute to a duct blockage.

Generally speaking, if you keep good tabs on how your breasts feel, get proactive when you do notice a possible clog, and avoid constricting them more than necessary, you can probably avoid mastitis.

Rise and shine

If you are a morning runner, you will inevitably confront the issue of what to do about nursing pre-run. Some mothers feel that they can run on full breasts without a problem, and others feel sore just thinking about that idea. Most likely, you'll either nurse or pump before your run, which can mean waking up earlier. If baby is an early riser, the decision is made for you! If not, and you don't want to wake baby up to nurse (trust me, we *all* understand if you don't - remember that adage about never waking a sleeping baby?) then there is always pumping. Assuming you have a spouse or someone else at home with baby during your run, they can always give a bottle of pumped milk while you are on your run.

There are countless strategies for this type of routine, and you will undoubtedly find one that works well for you!

Mighty Mama: Susan Empey

Age: 46

Home: Mercer Island, WA

Run Life: Runner for Oiselle Volée Team, 6 time USATF National Masters Champion, 2 time Olympic Trials Marathon Qualifier

Children: 13 year-old son and 15 year old daughter

The number one thing I noticed after having both children and getting back into running (which I did not do at all until I received the "all-clear" from my OBGYN -- 6 weeks post-delivery) was what a true pleasure running was. I quickly appreciated that the time I had allotted myself to run was a real gift and I treasured that time more than I ever had before. And the time I spent running, while some may say was selfish because it was time spent away from my child, I know with 100% certainty that I was a better mom and wife the days that I was able to run. Each run took on more significance because the time really mattered, so each

run I had a very specific plan and I truly enjoyed every minute I was out doing what I loved - on my own (I will say the times I did run with either child with the jog stroller that my hips got much stronger!)

My running became more focused and consequently more enjoyable than it ever had before and it really was after having kids that I probably earned the label of a "competitive runner." My best times and my biggest successes all came post children - which I think is partly attributed to the physiological changes that take place, partly because I was tougher after giving birth twice (labor was way more painful than any marathon I'd run!), and the time I spent running was generally more targeted to very specific goals. I did not have the extra time to monkey around!

One of the specific challenges I faced related to breastfeeding and training was after my 2nd child was born. I hoped to breastfeed for one year but wanted to run the Boston Marathon in April, and since he is an Independence Day baby - that meant I had to get back in marathon shape within 10 months - or really 8 1/2 months since I waited 6 weeks to get the all-clear from my doctor. I loved having the goal out there which was not necessarily to go after a PR, but just get myself fit enough that I could run confidently again.

I slowly began building up mileage and, I think, roughly 3 months into that training block, felt like I had enough of a base to begin some speed work. I made sure to hydrate extra well during that time, focused on eating healthy foods, and getting as much rest as one could with a toddler and baby in tow. But by the time Boston rolled around, I had confidence that I could string together 26.2 miles at a decent, but not record breaking clip. I think I ran about a 3:12, (which was at that time 18 minutes slower than my PR) but finished with a smile on my face.

But here was the challenging thing about running Boston while breastfeeding: because you have to get to the Athlete's Village so many hours before the actual race starts, and because, unless you're Kara Goucher, your marathon is at least 3 hours, that means at least 6 hours (if you're lucky) of not being able to breastfeed. I can literally see the change in my chest through race photos that by the time I crossed that finish line (it would be the one and only time I could have been hired at Hooters), I did not stop running and essentially ran right to the hotel, took the *absolute fastest shower I ever had, and hooked up my child faster than you can say "BOSTON MARATHON". I was a fire hose to that poor child, but it was only after that particularly satisfying session of feeding him that I took a deep breath and enjoyed the immense satisfaction of running that race.*

Some advice on a running while pregnant and post-pregnancy: absolutely listen to your body and when running does not feel good, especially when pregnant, that's when you stop and become a power walker instead. Every person carries their baby differently, and while it may be cool to be that woman who runs when she is 8 months pregnant, I don't think it means she is any tougher than the one who stops at 4 months. Power walking became a great form of exercise for me (as did swimming) when running just stopped feeling good. And I also would not start back to running a day before my doctor said it was ok to return. Starting back too early can just set you back in the long run, and again, power walking was a nice way to slowly but safely get back into running. And between that, eating well, and breastfeeding, my baby weight melted off. I enjoyed having bigger boobs and a slender body for a long time!

Chapter 12
Life As You Know It

This chapter probably applies more to new moms than seasoned veterans, but as the veterans can attest, every new edition to the family involves adjustment. The changes that come with welcoming a new baby into your life are significant, as we have thus far seen. What you might be somewhat less prepared for are the emotional changes that you may go through.

This is when running can be your best friend again. When you are adjusting to a new sleep schedule, when you are needing some time for yourself, or when you simply need a reminder of a part of yourself that you fear losing, running is there for you.

Why am I crying?
Your alarm goes off again. Remember, that alarm from Chapter 1? Yep, there it goes. 5:00 am. You swear it sounds more shrill and nagging than it used to. After hitting 'snooze' a couple of times, you finally begin to crawl across your bedroom to your running shoes.

Why did I put them way over here? You ask yourself.

Then your eyes drift shut, just a little, and your mind takes you back to that weird dream you were having before the alarm. You don't really remember what you did next, but you're walking down the hall when you open your eyes.

It's all you can do to get yourself to the living room.

Oh, that couch. It is so nice. Couches are so nice.

But your Garmin is on the other side of the room, and your feet somehow take you there instead. You wonder just how far muscle-memory goes, and in your groggy mind's eye, it briefly takes the form of a large, globular beast chasing you through that dream of yours.

Shoes are on. Garmin is on. Hat is on. Bra and tank are on. Shorts are…

Still in your bedroom. You consider starting your run anyways. It took a lot of effort to get to the front door. Besides, it's dark out. No one will notice you have no pants on. People run in competition briefs all the time. But no, no. Bad idea. Back to your bedroom you go.

You're pulling your shorts on while waddling back towards the door, grumbling an apology to your partner who was jerked awake when you tripped over the dresser drawer. Ready for real this time. And then...

"Eh heh...eh HEH...EH HEH....WAAAAAAAAAHHHHHH!"

Baby is awake. And hungry. Very hungry. Usually, your partner has morning duty while you run, but this time you didn't make it out the door in time. She keeps crying. If you get her and nurse, she will go ballistic if you try to leave. If you slip out the door and let the normal routine ensue, she will at least have consistency, and future morning runs won't be compromised.

That's what I'll do, you think, moving closer to the door. And then....

The pinch. On one side, and then the other. Then the damp. On both sides. Yep, the letdown. You had been at an impasse for only a matter of seconds before your breasts chose for you. The run will be too uncomfortable now. You turn off your Garmin, go to the nursery and greet your precious, screaming angel with a warm hug. Your partner is more than happy for a well-deserved sleep in.

Nursing is a wonderful time to tune-in to your baby and yourself, and this time you are hit by a wave of conflicting feelings: relief and guilt.

Relief that you aren't running right now, even though you used to love getting out there for your morning run. It is understandable. Baby girl work you up three times last night and you haven't had more than three hours of consecutive sleep since before your water broke. Yesterday's track workout was a doozy. You just started going back to work. You and your partner had an argument last night about the state of your sex lives since baby's birth. You're breastfeeding. You can't drink coffee all day because you're breastfeeding. You would kill for a massage. Exhausted doesn't even begin to describe it. You don't feel yourself anymore; you've been replaced by a listless zombie.

But that is why I run, your remind yourself. *My running keeps me sane. I need my running, now more than ever.*

Enter the guilt.

But my baby needs me, and that's more important.

My partner needs our intimacy back more so than I do. I'm not a good partner.

How can I take time to go running when it only benefits me? How selfish of me!

You punish yourself for not running enough and for running too much and believe that you're failing everyone in the process. You're a competitive runner, remember, and hence a perfectionist. In an effort to be solution-focused, you try to think of what would help you, and those you love most. But your mind is still trying to pull you back to that weird dream with the muscle-memory monster dancing the Macarena with your friend from high school. Too foggy, and now a bit dizzy.

You look down at your baby, how sweet and perfect she looks in your arms, how happy she is to be warmed by your body and draw milk from your breast, and her adorable murmurs of contentment.

It's all worth it for this, is the sensation that emanates through you from the inside out.

But as soon as your mind takes you back to your missed run, your daughter's nighttime waking, your frustrated partner, painful confusion ensues.

Why am I so unhappy?

The tears start to run down your cheeks. Fast at first, but they slow as they curve around your smile. You're still smiling at her.

Thanks, oxytocin.

I am sure that you, reader, have experienced some, most, or all of this.

You're not alone, mama.

Whether you breastfeed or not, whether you go back to work or stay at home, whether your baby immediately sleeps through the night or not, conflicting and even painful emotions can run rampant through your postpartum period. From a biological standpoint, this is due to the hormonal shifts that your body takes you through. As we discussed in Chapter 11, nursing moms often experience these shifts longer than those who wean early.

But it's not just the hormones. A roller-coaster of emotions can happen to anyone. Combine the effect of hormones with the changes in lifestyle that come with the addition of a family member and you've got an emotional storm brewing.

Changes abound

You're a competitive runner, so I'm going to wager that you are extremely organized in planning and anticipating the changes that baby brings. From nursery nesting to maternity leave to selecting a child care provider, you're prepared. One thing you may not have anticipated, at least not to the degree that it can affect you: the rapid rate at which these changes occur. For most of us, the life changes that manifest during the postpartum period tend to strike in one concentrated "oomph". Any one of these life changes are challenging enough to handle by themselves, let alone all at once. This can be more challenging to cope with than you might be ready for.

Mine created a perfect storm. When my son was 8 months old, my family made the move from California to Florida. We had lived there before, had many friends there, and my husband's family lived there. Since we made the decision that I would stay home with Jack until he is old enough for preschool, it made perfect sense to move back to Florida, to have a support network in a familiar place. I was certainly excited about this new adventure. I was reveling in every minute spend with my little guy, excited to get writing again, excited to reconnect with old friends, inspired with thoughts of taking Jack on adventures, and had all kinds of ideas for marine science projects in the education community. I would try to keep doing what I loved, with Jack at the helm of my time and attention, of course. Being a stay-at-home mom would be defined in my own way.

Everything sounded great in theory, but the reality was quite different. I had moved frequently throughout my life, so the change of venue didn't shake me. But the pace of my life and its emphasis, certainly did. Teaching science and coaching cross country is such a joy; I had been doing it since I graduated from college. Even though I was going to teach an online marine science class from home, things were definitely not going to be the same. I was the happiest in my California teaching life than I had ever been, professionally speaking, and that wonderful blink-of-an-eye chapter had ended. On top of that, with the reduction from two to one full-time salary, our budget tightened, which almost always causes relationship stress. I went from interacting with work colleagues and friends on a daily basis – we lived at a boarding school in California, and so had a built-in social life – to becoming fluent in baby babble and rarely leaving the house.

Though I was getting to visit with old friends, schedules and careers and life in general made it less frequent than I had expected (how dare they have lives!) I remember a stroller walk to Starbucks one day during which, while ordering, I realized that this barista was the first adult I had spoken with in three days, other than my husband. My own voice sounded weird to me. Don't get me wrong, I'm definitely not what you would call a "social butterfly". Actually, quite introverted. Yet I was lonely, and struggling to recognize myself in this new life. At least I still had my running!

Until I didn't. I overdid it, ran too hard, too soon. Maybe it was a subconscious coping mechanism. I incurred a lower back and hip injury within two months of moving back to Florida. Just in time for the fall racing season. Recovery took about six weeks – not long at all in the overall scheme of things, but at the time it was pure and simple hell. My career was on pause, my social life was not as vibrant as I had hoped, my husband and I argued at the drop of a hat, and then I couldn't run, or do anything athletic for that matter due to the nature of my injury. Did I mention that Jack was still waking up every two-three hours in the night?

I belittled myself constantly. Because all you ever hear from friends and family is how wonderful it is to watch your child grow and change, what a treasure parenthood is, and how quickly it ends, and how much you must enjoy it now, etc. And here I was, lucky enough to be able to stay at home with my child, even if it meant a tight budget for a few short years. Here I was, back in my college town with friends everywhere. Here I was, with this wonderful, funny, adventurous, smiling little boy with me all day. Here was my incredible husband, working his tail off teaching days, evening, and tutoring, to make ends meet so that I could be at home. How dare I be unhappy? How dare I let everyone down? What if I'm not even doing a good job raising Jack? What if it's all for nothing?

This is a very common mental trap to get stuck in during times of significant change, especially when that change affects your hormones.

Never underestimate the power of hormones.

Postpartum depression

Think back to your favorite race. One that you trained the hardest for and had the best possible result. Months of hard work went into it, anticipation kept you up at night, your friends and family didn't know you could be a giggly, bubbly nut until they saw you during your taper week. You felt the most alive you have ever felt on race day, and it paid off in spades. Success! You set a big PR, qualified for Boston, qualified for the Olympic Trials, or for the National Team, or maybe you won the World Championships. Whatever it was, *you did it, baby!* Celebration ensues. You return home, victorious. You start to relax and recover.

Now, what?

Many of us come down with a case of the "post-race blues" during this time. The reaching of any goal closes a chapter in our lives and can leave us feeling empty. Without this goal, what are we? This is precisely the case with the "baby blues", which is very common in the first few days postpartum. You are exhausted from delivery, relieved from delivery, perhaps nervous about being responsible for this tiny, screaming, pooping, adorable life, and are being hit with a flood of hormonal changes. The "baby blues" are not considered to be a severe condition, and usually go away within a few days as hormones and your new routine with baby begin to stabilize.

Baby blues are not to be confused with postpartum depression (PPD), which can start anytime within a year of delivering and is a serious mental health condition. Fathers can experience this too, just from the lifestyle change of new parenthood. The American Psychological Association reports that between 9% and 16% of postpartum women experience PPD, which rises to 41% among women who had PPD in the past.[23] Hormones are a *big* player in PPD, especially estrogen and progesterone. It is important to note that if a woman resumes a hormonal birth control method, one or both of these hormones can fluctuate pretty significantly and may be contributing to PPD symptoms. The range of symptoms is pretty large, anything from typical depression symptoms to intense anxiety and inability to function to thoughts of hurting oneself or baby. Professional intervention can be necessary, and recognizing the signs of possible PPD is the first and most important step.

If you are experiencing symptoms of PPD, you owe it to yourself and your baby to reach out to your doctor or a mental health professional.

There is no shame in having PPD.

None.

It does not make you a bad mother. It does not mean that you don't love your baby enough. It does not mean that you can't be happy. It does not mean that you are weak.

Reaching out is an act of strength.

Call your doctor.

Your doctor can give great advice for improving your condition, even if you are not officially diagnosed with PPD. Sometimes it's the small things in your daily routine that can make a big different on how you feel. These might include:

> *Carving out some "you time" each day to be alone in your own thoughts, relax, read, anything that is just for you.*

---

[23] The APA has some great resources and statistics on PPD.

Taking turns attending to baby in the night with your partner, if you aren't already so that you can get more substantial sleep.

Calling a trusted friend or family member to come be with baby when you suddenly feel overwhelmed.

Getting together with a local "mom's group" a couple of times a week for any activity you choose, to talk and connect with other moms who may be experiencing the same thing.

If your doctor has given you the OK to return to running, getting back into a running routine and set a small goal for yourself.

Your doctor may also recommend prescription medication to help manage your depression. There are also foods that can have mood-elevating properties; these include foods rich in Omega-3 fatty acids (fish, nuts, flax), beets or beet sugar, and dark chocolate, thank goodness!

There are many different effective ways to treat PPD and they vary widely from woman to woman. The most important thing is to address the issue. Involve your partner and your family, to the extent that you feel comfortable, in helping you move through it. Don't be a martyr and try to ignore your feelings, thinking that in doing so you are putting baby's needs first. Baby needs a healthy mommy.

With respect to your running, it certainly can help improve your baby blues or PPD or down feelings. Not only because you are doing what you enjoy and are passionate about, but because of the endorphin release. Just don't let running become another stressor. Set modest running goals, run by feel rather than by your watch, run for fun. There will be another time for pushing your limits and it's not too far away. Right now, your mind and body need your running to be pure enjoyment.

Use running to improve your mind rather than focus your mind on improving your running.

> **Need help? Call the PPD Moms Project:**
> # 1-800-PPD-MOMS
> (773-6667)
> www.1800ppdmoms.org

Body image

As you settle into your new life with baby, and you get accustomed to all that has changed, you slowly regain some of the little "normalcies" of your pre-baby days. Friends come over again, the next season of your favorite TV show resumes, you can run again, you can leave baby with a sitter or family member while you go on an actual date with your partner beyond the grocery store. However small or big they are, you realize that your life isn't *completely* upended. And the ways in which it has changed can be wonderful beyond what you might have expected.

Then you look in the mirror. Maybe you have avoided it since delivery, or maybe you've checked your naked self out in fascination every day. Your body is not the same as before you were pregnant. Nor should it be! You used it to make a human. Your body deserves a medal of honor. Focus on these victories.

Don't focus, for one minute, on how you think you are *supposed* to look postpartum.

Don't think, even for a second, about the idiotic magazines that pour endless praise over celebrity moms whose bodies look "amazing" after just having a baby. Way too much emphasis and glorification is thrust upon this notion that you have succeeded at life if your body shows zero evidence of having given birth. Don't take the bait.

Don't belittle that incredible body of yours, not once, not at all.

Trust that with time, regaining your running regimen, and chasing around that little one as he/she becomes mobile, you will eventually get your pre-baby body back. And when you do, it will be so much stronger *because of what it looks like right now.*

New sex life

Sex can become complicated for any couples postpartum; add running into the mix and it can be like having a third wheel in the relationship. The last thing you want is to feel like you are between a rock and a hard place (zero puns intended there) when it comes to running and intimacy, two important elements of your life that have the potential to play tug-o-war with your limited time and energy during the first few months with a new baby.

It's possible that you're reading this thinking "Psssshhht. No problem with sex here." If so, awesome! Read no further.

There is a better chance, though, you're reading this and thinking "who can possibly think about or want sex when you've got a new baby to care for?" New mothers can have vastly different experiences with their sex drive in the postpartum weeks and months, complicated further by breastfeeding. Hormones are once again at the helm, and taking you on another wild ride through rapids.

For the first few weeks, whether you had a vaginal birth or a c-section, your doctor will recommend no sex until after that first appointment. You may not feel up to it physically for more days or weeks beyond that; everyone will handle it differently. Even once you are physically healed and ready for action, there are two hormones in your system that can greatly impact your sexual desire: oxytocin and prolactin, both of which we have previously discussed.

When you nurse your baby, oxytocin surges through your system, providing a sensation of love and closeness. It's a kind of "bonding hormone" that is also released during and immediately after sexual intercourse. Beautiful, isn't it? A hormone dedicated to stimulating feelings of love and connection. With all the nursing you're doing, you're getting so much oxytocin that you may not feel that you *need* to get it from sex.

Combine this with having a tiny human physically attached to you for so much of the day, constantly needing your body, it's understandable to not want *more* touching from your partner once the little one is asleep. Of course, this doesn't mean that you love your partner less or don't want their affection, just that you need your space.

The other hormonal culprit is prolactin. This is the hormone that stimulates lactation, and also keeps ovulation at bay for most of the time you are breastfeeding. Another interesting thing about prolactin: it is also released in men and non-nursing women during an orgasm. There have been many studies linking elevated prolactin levels in men to problems with sexual desire and intimacy. Why? Because prolactin essentially replaces the need for orgasm. For nursing moms, prolactin can be doing the same thing, and so further distancing them from needing sex.

If you experience a drop in sexual desire, beyond the first few weeks of healing, it can be a frustrating time for you and your partner. Add the fact that you might be resuming your running routine and you might unknowingly create a rivalry between your significant other and your running.

This can really present a challenge. On one hand, resuming your running makes you feel more like yourself again. It is your constant, your meditation, your defining activity that you resented being without while healing after delivery or during pregnancy itself. On the other hand, your partner has sexual needs and desires that have not necessarily changed and wants to feel close and connected to you. Both of you are probably lacking quality sleep, and if you've returned to work, there's another demand on your time and energy. Your partner may be wondering how you have the energy and desire to lace up your running shoes and dart out the door at o-dark-thirty, but don't have the energy or desire for sex.

Whatever your feelings and desires are in the first postpartum months, be patient and compassionate with yourself and your partner. Recognize that their needs are just as valid as your own, even if baby places more demands on you.

Let your running take your mind back to your love of the sport, your goals, and your pre-baby warrior self; that itself might help rebuild your desire for sex.

Communicate your feelings with your partner and be honest about each other's needs. The good news is that changes in your sex drive are most likely temporary; don't let this temporary change do permanent harm to your relationship. Feeling guilty or trapped by the many demands on your life is not healthy for either of you or for baby. Don't be afraid to seek out a counseling professional, if need be!

Back to work?

Many moms return to work when baby is a couple of months old, maybe more and maybe less. This can be a challenging time, too, for you and baby. You are accustomed to having baby on or near you all day long, and baby is accustomed to unlimited mommy access. When this dynamic changes, it definitely involves a transition period. Work will feel different. You might need to pump during the work day. You might miss your little one so much that work doesn't feel as enjoyable as it did before. You might feel overwhelmed by the needs of others.

Running can be helpful during this period as means of ensuring "you" time, when it may feel like your time is otherwise in constant demand. Let it take on this role, but be sure to ease into it with your new work routine. Changing too many factors in your life at once can be a recipe for stress and tension that you and your family really don't need. Maybe hold off on training hard for several weeks, to ensure that your mind and body are adjusting at the pace that they need to. Let running be first, and foremost, a source of fun in your otherwise busy life. Perhaps taking baby with you in the jogging stroller on some of your runs will give you more time with him or her.

> *Remember that there is no set timeframe for transitioning into life with a new baby.*
>
> *Be patient with you goals.*
>
> *Be compassionate with your family.*
>
> *Be responsive to your needs.*

Be grateful for every minute with your new baby! You run fast, mama, but so does time.

Mighty Mama: Pila Cadena

Age: 58

Home: St Petersburg, FL

Profession/Run Life: Store Manager at Fit-2-Run St Petersburg, running and fitness coach, marathoner, cancer survivor, local hero.

Children: Two grown kids, Erika & Justin

Did you run when you were pregnant with your kids? If so, how did it go?

Yes, I did. My first child, Erika, used to love riding in the stroller. I remember every time I stopped, she would ask for "more". With my son Justin, I faced an entirely different challenge. During my pregnancy, I was diagnosed with thyroid cancer and the doctors said we would have to terminate my pregnancy in order to commence radiation treatment. I *couldn't possibly imagine doing this; it was against my personal and religious principles. So my treatment was postponed until after Justin was born. Having two healthy, wonderful children was a big part of what kept me going during the exhausting and often debilitating process of fighting cancer; when I felt like I couldn't keep fighting, I knew I had to stay strong and push through for them. Running was the other part, the part that kept me fighting for <u>me</u>. It became my "light at the end of the tunnel", my little glimmer of strength and hope in myself.*

How did your running life change when you became a mom?

Tremendously, especially because there was no support from my [ex] husband. While I was battling cancer, he didn't know what to do or how to handle it, so he mostly shut down. I had no family close by during that time aside from my mother-in-law. It was a very lonely time for me, but running has a way of turning alone-time into strength, and I needed to fight for that strength in my life. My runs had to take place at 4:30am before anyone got up!

How has being a coach changed your running life?

In many ways, of course. It has been very rewarding, but my training, for myself, fell behind. As I am getting older it has become harder and harder to get it back.

What is the best thing about coaching and being highly involved in the running community?

Coaching has been a great highlight in my life. Being able to take someone from step one all the way to marathon training is amazing! Hard work, persistence, patience, tolerance, faith, have been the greater denominators while on this journey.

How have your running goals changed over the years?

Realizing and accepting the fact that I enjoy training others. My goals are just to get out every day and enjoy every step that I take. After surviving cancer, I've become more relaxed about life. I am enjoying the journey! Of course, there is always that competitor side of me that wants to get better and better. Working on it now!

PART IV – YOU SUCCEEDING

"I don't think I would have been such a good runner if I hadn't enjoyed it." - *Greta Waitz*

Chapter 13
Getting Faster

Things are about to get seriously fun. You have this wonderful baby in your life. You have hopefully struck a healthy balance between your personal, professional, and running goals. Your body is recovering or has fully recovered, from your pregnancy, and you are primed for making your running life really take flight.

You also have something within you now that was not there pre-baby: more resilience, more strength, and more gratitude for what running brings you. That gratitude is important, because it will allow you to enjoy your running in ways you might have previously taken for granted. This is a critical component of becoming a faster runner. I am excited for you, mama!

Chasing improvement
There will be important milestones in your running when you start seriously racing again: your first 5K post-baby, your first marathon post-baby, hitting about the same times as you did post-baby, and so on. Being a competitive runner, you eventually want to see your race times become faster than your pre-baby times.

As you chase your PRs, keep in mind that improvement doesn't always happen the way we want it to. As a coach, I have seen many cross country and track runners struggle with this concept. There's the occasional middle school phenom who peaks by sophomore year but then gets hit with the puberty truck and pains to understand why her body won't perform as well as it used to. This happens with girls more than boys. Suddenly acquiring boobs and a butt can definitely cramp your athletic style. You may remember going through this yourself: the intense frustration of not improving as you expected, especially if you watch a genetically-lucky teammate who still wears an A-cup break the school record or win the state championship. Novice runners come to quickly learn that improvement is rarely linear, and each subsequent race may not be faster than the last.

But that is a key part of the challenge: the unpredictability, the universe's dose of randomness, and the remote variables that cannot be controlled. Course conditions. Weather. Humidity. Hormones. Indigestion. Recovery speed. The list goes on, and the longer the distance raced, the more that hard work and preparation can be stealthily infringed upon by luck.

Fear of not setting a PR at a certain race or not hitting the benchmarks of improvements that you set for yourself can be your worst enemy as you move forward in your running career. It can cause you to ignore warning signs of impending injury or skip recovery days. Pushing your body too hard now *might* result in one or two fast races, if you don't get injured during that time, but could hijack your long-term ability to race by making you more injury-prone.

Yes, of course, hard workouts break our muscles down temporarily and recovery days allow them to heal stronger. Physiological stress is necessary. But therein lies a fine line between stimulating a positive adaptation in your training and overdoing it. You most likely know where that line is.

Ask yourself before *every single run* one critical question: will this workout make me stronger, or weaker, in the *long-term*?

The single key to improvement in distance running is patience. Simply, patience.

Your body just grew a human! It is clearly awesome. Trust it to guide you through your new running journey.

Gene machine

The first time I ran the Lilac City Bloomsday Race, I was eight years old. There were *huge* crowds of people at the start in their color-designated waves. Being a kid, naturally I pestered my mother about why we had to wait to start, why there were different waves at the start, and who got to start first. She explained to me that the fastest runners started at the front, mostly those speedy men and women from Kenya and Ethiopia. When I asked her why they were so fast, she replied "it's in their genes."

At that time in my life, I had been obsessed with whales and dolphins, and so had spent hours combing through National Geographic issues and

Encyclopedia Brittanica volumes on all things biology. I generally understood that genes were the blueprints of our physical features and behaviors and the reason why my brother and I resembled our parents. But I had never considered that genes could be responsible for a predisposition to running. I just figured the fastest runners were the ones who practiced the most. As it turns out, both concepts are correct.

The relationship between genes and the environment has interesting and dynamic implications for athletes. It was long thought that genetics plays the greatest role in athletic performance, and when genetic potential is evident, success can be predicted to a large-degree. It is frequently assumed that distance runners of East Africa have a distinctive genetic advantage over other ethnic groups.

The more we learn about genetics – particularly, how the environment can permanently alter gene expression – the more we have to re-evaluate this notion. A compilation of studies published in 2011 by the International Olympic Committee has analyzed all existing data on genetic influences in athletic performance, particularly in endurance sports.[24] Its findings show that the keys to exceptional athletic performance is an incredibly complex and highly individualized blend of genetics, environment, and training stimuli timing. It takes a village! And in the case of East African elite runners, it literally takes a village. Many have grown up running everywhere, every day, all the time. The villages they live in are running-centered, and the entire community supports training their fastest, highest performing runners to make it to the top of world championships and Olympic races. This makes a big case for "nurture" above "nature".

But environment and genetics do not exist in separate little vacuums. As the body changes in response to its environment, physiological adaptations take place to ensure its continued functioning under those

---

[24] Boucherd & Hoffman report in Chapter 31 on Genetic Advantage & Talent Selection: "...*athletes with a favorable genetic profile who interact with a favorable, matched training environment are more likely to achieve higher levels of performance. But the likelihood remains that the possible unique combinations of genetic and environmental factors resulting in elite-level performance are enormous and generally unpredictable.*"

conditions, which actually alters gene expression. One amazing example of physiological adaptation is mitochondria, the little "powerhouses" found in every single one of our cells, including our muscle tissue. They may look like nothing more than little red jelly beans under a high-powered microscope, but they are constantly using oxygen and food to churn out usable, mechanical energy that causes our muscles to contract. Sports physiology has shown us that more mitochondria means better aerobic performance, and the world's best endurance athletes all have a very high mitochondrial density. But they were not necessarily blessed with such mito-mighty cells. You can make more mitochondria through training, and when this happens, it alters the mitochondrial gene expression.[25] That's right, training can change your genes!

This does not mean, however, that inherited genes are not relevant. It just means that a genetically-blessed Scandanavian, Brazilian, Thai, American, or what-have-you, can be just as successful in the sport as a genetically-blessed Kenyan or Ethiopian, all other variables being equal. Training cannot create genes that weren't there in the first place. But it can certainly influence the *expression* of certain genes that affect aerobic capacity, muscle fatigue, oxygen transport, and a myriad of other physiological factors.

Your body is truly an incredible marvel of nature, intrinsically wired to maximize its potential under conditions that foster it. Your genes both determine "you", and are determined by what you do. The world's best athletes are born *and* made.

Your genes may bless you with some excellent muscle fiber ratios, or inherently high VO2 Max, or stabilizing bone structure. Or they may give you none of these. Our genetic talents don't always match our interests and the effort that one person must exert in their training compared to another to get the same end result is never equal or "fair".

---

[25] Boucherd & Hoffman report in Chapter 19: Mitochondrial DNA Sequence Variation and Performance: *"...mitochondrial function is strongly associated with energy status in muscle cells and with muscle performance. Mitochondria respond to muscle activity and training by adjusting both the number of mitochondria in myofibers, and the gene expression of the mitochondria."*

But next time you see who is towing the starting line at Boston or the Olympics, know that there, too, is a spectrum of genetic ability. Yes, they all clearly have *some* genetic predisposition, but they also differ in age, how long they have been runners, coaching, access to sports medicine resources, sponsorship and "day-job" dynamic, and more. Environment influences genetics. If you're not born with optimized genes for running, you can still maximize and improve what you *do* have.

For me, personally, the science of genetics and training helps to formulate my overall training mantra: to fulfill my genetic potential as a runner. I can't control what genes I was born with, but there are many factors that I *can* control in maximizing my success, and my gene expression! I relish in the challenge of learning, adapting, and implementing variables that improve my running. Whether this journey takes me to the Olympic Trials or simply to new PRs, I will do the very best my genes, environment, and lifestyle will allow. This mindset towards training goals really improves my sense of perspective. While you may not find it as meaningful in framing your training paradigm, I hope that at least it serves as a useful angle with which to consider yourself as a runner.

Setting the bar high

It is for the reasons just described that we really should avoid setting goals based upon the performance of others, especially elites. Yes, Paula Radcliffe won the New York City Marathon ten months postpartum. But that does not mean that you should expect a similar magnitude of success so soon after pregnancy. Remember that, for many of the elites, running is their job. Their training and sponsorship are such that they have access to technologies and physical therapies that most runners likely do not. That is not to say that we can't, but most of us don't have the facility access to an anti-gravity treadmill.

You might be dealt a pleasant surprise; as we have seen in previous chapters about the physiological advantages that postpartum running can bring, there are several reasons why many women set PRs in the months following pregnancy. But setting your heart on a very specific or ambitious goal soon after delivering might cause you to ignore warning signs that your body isn't quite ready.

Many runners like to return to a training plan that they have used before and were successful with. This can have some substantial psychological benefits: it is familiar, and you *know* you can succeed with it. But at the same time, your body is operating under different conditions than it was prior to pregnancy. Flexibility is key! Starting with a familiar training plan may be a good move, just make sure you are willing to adjust as needed. No rigidity.

The biggest point I want to emphasize here is, again, patience. By all means, you should set high goals for yourself! You can do incredible things with your body; don't sell yourself or your dreams short. Just be realistic about the timeline. Qualifying for Boston six months after you give birth might land you injured before you can race; qualifying for Boston in the next two years might be a very achievable yet equally badass goal. You have *much* more time ahead of you to do incredible things as a runner than you might think you do – and you'll want to be *healthy* through all of those years.

The best is yet to come

Every year that I have coached track and cross country, I had a conversation with the seniors just before their final meet about their futures as runners. The perpetual celebration of transition that comes with senior year tends to focus on what is ending: high school classes, sports, clubs, living at home with parents, all things tied to teenage-hood. For most athletes, in most sports, this is true. Unless they are moving on to college with an athletic scholarship to play their sport, graduating from high school most likely closes the competitive athletic chapter of their lives. And unless the college athletes go professional, they will go through the same closure in another four years. It is a very emotional time, especially for those whose new and developing identities were closely tied to their athletic pursuits. There is usually a last game, match, or race: "senior night", where the teams exalt their leaders at the end of their athletic careers.

What I emphasized to my athletes: distance running is different.

Competitive running is very much a lifetime sport. It can be picked up at any time, taken as seriously as you want it to be, have a wide variety of purposes in your life, be dropped, and be picked back up. You can be part of a team, or not. You can run races, or not. You can use it simply to stay healthy, or train for another sport, or as a way to bond with friends, or not.

Unlike just about every other competitive sport, the fastest long-distance runners in the world do *not* peak in their late teens to early twenties. If you watch the world championships or Olympics, you will see an interesting progression of age from the sprints and short distance track events to the longer races, especially the marathon.

Marathon runners tend to peak in their late twenties, maybe early thirties, but even older runners are finding themselves among the top ten men and women in the world's most prestigious races. In 2014, American Meb Keflezki won the Boston Marathon at age 38, the first American man to win Boston in 15 years. He beat runners who were ten, fifteen, twenty years his junior. Based on the pervasive assumption that 'younger' means 'stronger' and 'faster', and that age ticks away on an athlete's peak potential, dozens of elite men in that race should have beaten Meb.

For women, this age inversion can be even more staggering. In the 2008 Summer Olympics in Beijing, the women's marathon field was lead by Americans Deena Kastor and Magdalena Lewy Boulet, both 35 at the time, and won by Constantina Tomescu-Dita of Romania, a 38-year old mom who had only completed ten marathons prior to the Olympics! It goes to show that to perform optimally in this sport, one's fitness accumulates after many years of training, and the physical resilience demanded by long distance running ages like a fine wine.

That having been said, there is a fine balance to strike between accumulated fitness and wear-and-tear. No matter how physically strong she is, there are definite and unavoidable changes that aging brings to an endurance athlete. Even the fittest and fastest will experience a steady decline in VO2 max, and have to work harder at retaining muscle mass.

The drop in VO2 max puts a ceiling on your maximum aerobic capacity, so if you have spent most of your life performing at your maximum possible VO2 max, your performance will slowly begin to drop, or at least be more difficult to attain the same level of effort.[26] In 2014, Deena Kastor – at 41 years old - set the World Master's Record in the Half Marathon with a time of 1:09:36, two full minutes slower than her all-time Half Marathon PR and National (non-masters) record of 1:07:34. She set her all-time PR when she was 33. Even though she can no longer out-run her younger self, she still sets world records in the sport and her competitive life continues to be enriched.

The running community recognizes the changes brought by aging, which is why a Master's league exists. If you're approaching 40, get excited to cultivate a whole new set of PRs!

On the flip side, they won't *necessarily* be slower times. If you started competitive running later in life, you may have yet to perform consistently at your VO2 max and can still improve and set all-time PRs, even as that max starts to decline with age. Someone who has been competitively running for ten years, regardless of their age, will also have less "wear and tear" on their running bodies than someone who has been competitively running for twenty years. It's all relative, and what you get out of your running *will* change throughout your life, especially when you become a parent.

---

[26] This study by Quinn et al, in the Journal of Strength and Conditioning Research, measured all variables affecting running performance: oxygen uptake (VO2 max), lactate threshold, muscle strength, body composition, muscular power, and flexibility. It found that the decrease in performance was not due to a decrease in running economy (efficiency), but instead due to a decrease in VO2 max and muscular power. Good news – muscular power can be improved through training!

Mighty Mama: Sue Iverson Casaway

Age: 63

Home: Scottsdale, AZ

Profession: Database administrator for Brophy Preparatory School in Phoenix

Run Life: Age-group triathlon champ and perpetual supporter of others in her athletic community (fun fact: she also convinced me to run cross country when I was in high school!)

Children: Two grown sons, Peter (35) and Eric (33)

Sue with me (left) and with her granddaughter, Stella (right).

Did you run when you were pregnant with your kids? If so, how did it go?

My running days began in my early twenties, with plenty of hills and valleys along the way. We're talking 1973 here, so road-running was still new for the general population/non-track athletes. Nike Waffles, fruit juices, and Ju-Ju-Bes candy were my personal choice for road shoes, electrolyte drinks, and energy gels/blocks/power bars in these early years.

Nutrition wasn't a priority for runners yet, as long as you drank plenty of water, you're good to go! I did continue to run in the early '80s while pregnant from 4 - 9 months. During those first three months, I only felt good in the swimming pool. Living in Sacramento, CA in the summer humidity and heat were just too much for me. Seems the lap-swimming was all I could do to get my workouts going. I was worried about overheating by core temperature, but once the weather cooled off, I was back out there running, doing what I loved to do, just for me and baby #1! My most memorable run while pregnant was running a 6 mile race at 6 months, with baby belly in full bloom, wearing a loose t-shirt announcing "I should have been running" with a Baby On Board arrow down to my belly. That shirt kept me smiling for miles!

How did your running life change when you became a mom?

Once my first son was born, I was determined to not slow down or quit running. I think that's really important for a young mom - to still find time for yourself and get your workouts in. That mind-body connection was stronger than ever for me, even as I nursed for 10 months, I had a goal of running 10 miles again, so found a running buddy and we slowly upped the mileage. I have to admit, my speed racing days were over, but just being out there a few times a week made all the difference. Some new moms are fortunate to get their speed back, but I'm sure I just didn't push myself as hard as before. My priorities changed. Running was still my love and escape for 'Me time", but the clock didn't seem to matter nearly as much.

What is the best thing about connecting with your running community?

Over the years, my running days have come and gone, and now come back to one-third of my training. I ventured into triathlons about 10 years ago and have never looked back. I have an amazing community of triathletes, both men and women, most much younger than me. We meet for hill runs, long runs, bike rides, and open water swims - always followed by coffee, breakfast, and plenty of laughs. We're in various tri-clubs, running clubs, and fitness clubs. I simply cannot imagine training on my own anymore, or doing just one sport. If I want the peace and quiet of a solo run, bike or swim, that's always an option, but my focus has become more on the comradery and friendships of my training partners that have grown and *developed over the last 10 years. There is such a rich, personal bond that develops with those you chat with over the long miles and coffee that you cannot replace. We are young mothers, career women, single, married/re-married, divorced, and grandmothers and granddads, with new stories every week!*

How have your running goals changed over the years?

At 63 years young, my running/triathlon goals are nothing like in my twenties. Since there are so few of us in my age-group, I always have a fighting chance to make the podium in many local races. I don't feel the need to travel out of state too often, as Arizona has more than enough races year-round. I enjoy the shorter races now (Sprint or Olympic) and have only done one Half-Ironman (70.3 miles of swimming/cycling/running). The Ironman distance (140.6 miles) fever has not gripped me yet, but who knows if I'll try it in my '70s! I am still a bit competitive when racing others in my age group, but please don't compare my times with a young 30-50 something! It's all about the finish line, still smiling, feeling accomplished, and knowing I've pushed myself just hard enough to earn that ice-cold beer or latte that's waiting for me.

Any advice for new running moms out there?

My best advice to any new running mom is to be patient, listen to your own body, and explain to your husband/partner the importance of 'Me Time' which will absolutely make you a much happier Mom!! You need your family's support, love, and encouragement to keep running without guilt, but rather the freedom and joy that comes with a good run. Just realize that life is ever-changing, so stay flexible (yes, do your Yoga), and keep moving forward!

Chapter 14
Staying Healthy

This is, perhaps, the most important chapter of this book. Injury prevention is at the heart of my decision to research and document my own experiences. And I would wager that it is a major reason why many running mamas and mamas-to-be jump on the interwebs and Amazon bookstore to find resources in their own training. For longevity in this sport, it is necessary.

To us running devotees, pregnancy poses an entirely new spectrum of injury risk that goes beyond the standard cautionary wisdom. But do not dread or fear this! Becoming a new mother is an amazing process worth cherishing and enjoying, and the changes your body undergoes comes with some surprising benefits for your running. Once you understand the types of physiological changes you can expect, as we discussed in Parts II and III, you will be armed and equipped to navigate through prenatal and postpartum training.

This chapter will address concepts of injury prevention and healthful training that go beyond the topic of pregnancy and new motherhood, so bear with me as we venture somewhat off topic into a subject that *all* runners need to confront.

We are not invincible

Most statistics on running injury all show that about 70% of runners of *all* abilities will become injured during their running careers.[27] These include minor and major injuries. If you're a highly competitive athlete, you are exerting a greater, more frequent stress on your body than a recreational runner is. You're also probably more likely to try running through an injury. These factors would suggest that higher-performing, more

---

[27] Data taken from the American Academy of Physical Medicine and Rehabilitation, *"Runners of All Types Prone to Injuries"*, Musculoskeletal resources, 2015

competitive runners are more likely to be injured than recreational athletes. But statistics on running injury actually say otherwise!

A 2013 article published in the *Orthopedic Journal of Sports Medicine* analyzed injury risk among 930 novice runners to see what factors were most closely tied to injury. Most of the injury risk factors they identified were pretty intuitive: a BMI greater than 30, a previous injury not related to running, and 45 – 65 years of age. One other factor I found to be particularly interesting: having an easygoing, non-competitive personality was tied to an *increased* risk of injury. In this study, controlling for the other variables studied, the runners who were identified as "Type A" personalities in psychological testing endured fewer injuries than the runners who were identified as "Type B".[28] Granted, this is just one study.

But let's ask anyway: how could this be? Aren't we hypercompetitive Type-A runners more inclined to push ahead of everyone else during a group run and strain our hamstrings while sprinting past each other? Or after not winning a race, going home and tackling more intense workouts than we should be able to handle to make that big comeback in next week's 5K? Especially as novice runners.

Runner's World online writer Scott Douglas suggests that the more competitive novice runners might be more focused and in-tune with their bodies during a run, while a less competitive novice runner may have their minds elsewhere and could miss their body's warning signs when a pain creeps in.[29] Being novice, both groups of runners have likely not reached the point of choosing to ignore warning signs when they fear impending injury, a characteristic that could eventually be adopted by the competitive types.

I suggest a different hypothesis: that the competitive rookies are more likely to have a stronger musculoskeletal baseline than the less-competitive rookies; as a result of their competitive nature, the Type-A are more likely to have engaged in other athletic activity in the past, and

---

[28] From the OJSM, May 2 2013, *Predictors of Running-Related Injuries Among 930 Novice Runners: A 1-year prospective follow-up study* by Nielsen et al.
[29] This study was also referenced on *Runner's World* online 'Newswire' in May of 2013 by Scott Douglass, *Risk Factors for Injury in New Runners*.

thus have a somewhat more resilient structure. Or, perhaps the competitive types are more likely to engage in dynamic and static stretching before and after their runs since they are taking their performance more seriously than their laid-back compatriots.

Whatever the reason, this study serves as an example of a very important takeaway for us competitive types trying to avoid injury: *it's the "extraneous" stuff that matters the most.*

Whether paying attention to your body's signals during a run, or strength and resistance training or implementing static and dynamic drills into your routine, your risk of injury can be greatly reduced.

This is good news! It means that injury is not some random occurrence that strikes you in the midst of your training without warning or cause. You *can* take action to prevent it.

Safety first

Just as in the field of medicine as a whole, there are two key aspects to injury prevention:

1. Preventative maintenance

2. Recognizing signs of impending doom, and taking action

Generally speaking, most runners need to improve at both of these. When we are crunched for time, it becomes easy to skip doing dynamic drills before runs, our strength training routines, proper warm-up, and cool-downs, or our post-run stretching. And as intricately attuned we are to our bodies, when a potential injury creeps into our pain receptors, we quickly turn into toddlers with fingers in our ears screaming *"LA LA LA CAN'T HEAR YOU!"*

To have a long, successful career in running, it is crucial to change this mindset.

Many of us were lucky enough to not suffer many injuries in our earlier years of running, which has lulled us into a false sense of security when it comes to the importance of injury prevention. We haven't had to worry about it in the past, so why worry now? What about that old saying: *if it's not broke, don't fix it?*

After years of sustained, intense training cycles, the actual saying changes: *if it's not broke, it very well might be soon.* Maybe that sounds a bit pessimistic, and certainly not necessarily true of ALL runners. But given that 70% of runners DO suffer injuries at some point in their running careers, it's not far off. We are all aging, whether we like it or not, and wear n' tear does eventually happen.

Given all of the physiological strains and changes that come with pregnancy, as we saw in Parts II and III, aging is not the only culprit behind running injuries. Pregnancy can drastically increase your susceptibility to injuries, both pre and post-natal, and the caution you imagine only much older runners having to take suddenly applies to you too.

Exposing dysfunction

As I mentioned before, I managed to injure my hip muscles twice within a year of my son's birth, both times after pushing my training too hard. Interestingly, both injuries manifested themselves when I hit 40 miles per week, which is about 10 miles per week less than I had been accustomed to running pre-pregnancy. After three months of working with Dr. Maggio (see my interview with him at the end of this chapter) and finally getting some real strength back in my hips, back, glutes, and hamstrings, I winced as I completed another 40 mile week...but this time, pain-free and feeling stronger than ever, as I have since then. My form is better. My stride is so much more powerful. My gait is more efficient. Everything about how my body runs is different now. When I started racing again, hitting PR's in every distance from the 10K to the marathon, I remember feeling a profound sense of gratitude for the weakness my body experienced postpartum, and yes, even for the injuries.

How can a runner possibly be *glad* for her injuries?

Those injuries exposed dysfunction in my running form that I didn't even know was there. They uncovered chronic weaknesses in my hips, hamstrings, and back that my body merely tolerated through hard training but were revealed after my pregnancy. Those weaknesses were injuries waiting to happen, long before my pregnancy. They were ticking time bombs that might have actually caused permanent damage had I never realized their presence.

Pain is your body's way of letting you know when something needs fixing. It is not a weakness, but a critical warning system. It forces you to rest and to take injury prevention much more seriously. Maybe that is the bigger lesson for all athletes, pregnant or not, male or female. You don't need a pregnancy to realize, address, and treat possible weaknesses in your physique. You need only become more proactive about injury prevention than you [most likely] are right now. If you do incur and injury, view it as an opportunity to improve yourself as an athlete. That is pretty powerful silver lining if you ask me.

Healing habits

You know the little stickers that auto mechanics put in your car windshield after it was serviced, to let you know when the next oil change is needed? You don't need to worry about your car engine functioning properly, unless a 'check engine' light goes on, until the next service. If maintenance on our bodies was this easy, there would be far fewer injured runners out there. While a serious runner might see their sports doctor every so often during intense training cycles for a "tune-up", preventing injuries is something she must engage in well beyond doctor's visits. It requires consistent effort, every run.

The ability to do this successfully is dependent upon the forming of "anti-injury habits". Once implemented, they eventually become mindless second-nature. *That* is when your chances of incurring an injury drop way, way down. These habits include:

Proper warm-up and cool down before and after running

Dynamic drills before hard workouts

Stretching after hard workouts

The use of foam rollers or other self-massage devices

Epsom salt baths after hard workouts

These types of habits treat your soft tissues: muscles, tendons, ligaments, and fascia. After intense workouts, such tissues become inflamed. Muscle tissue breaks down so that it rebuilds itself stronger; this is why we do hard workouts. Tendons and ligaments are significantly worked in the process. Fascia stretches to accommodate the wide ranges of movement that your running parts must achieve.

All of these things are *good*...if, and only if, they heal properly. Rest heals because it allows time for critical nutrients to be delivered to the damaged tissue for rebuilding. Think of your circulatory system as a network of roads bringing building supplies to a construction site. By engaging in the soft tissue habits shown above, you are accelerating the rate of nutrient delivery to those damaged tissues. You're increasing the speed limit on the roads to the construction site, and insisting that the cargo trucks drive faster! This facilitates recovery and decreases your body's inflammatory response.

The inflammatory response can be positive in some ways – the entire reason it exists is to deliver immune cells ("reinforcements", if you will) to the site of trauma, tissue stress, or infection. This can include the construction of scar tissue, which works kind of like temporary scaffolding on buildings to support and reinforce the muscle tissue while it is repaired.

The problem with scar tissue is that it interferes with proper muscle contraction; if you continue working those muscles hard, they don't get a chance to rebuild. By jamming muscle fiber contraction, the scar tissue causes you pain long after the inflammatory response has stopped.[30]

This is why we cannot successfully train at hard intensities *all the time*. We need recovery days of only easy or no running, recovery weeks of lightened intensity and mileage, and every so often, recovery months after a series of intense training cycles. Through the practices of stretching, massaging, and generally promoting blood flow and relaxation of your muscles post-workout, you are essentially beating the inflammatory response to the punch. You get all the goods of inflammation (nutrients for rebuilding muscle tissue) minus the problematic elements (scar tissue build-up). Recovery allows our muscles to "de-stress", stop being inflamed all the time, and to rebuild stronger.

---

[30] Delayed Onset Muscle Soreness (DOMS) is a common occurrence for athletes, and is usually the result of sudden inflammation.

Quality materials

For your muscles to rebuild themselves, it is important that they have high-quality building materials. You can't build a quality house out of straw; just ask the Three Little Pigs. You need materials that can withstand many more huffs and puffs than what the Big Bad Wolf has to dish out. For your muscles, this material is protein.

When it comes to nutrition, endurance athletes tend to focus more on carbohydrates, since they are the primary fuel source that power our performance. For the longer-distance runners, fats tend to take the silver as providing long-lasting energy while holding off carb burning, hence avoiding "hitting the wall". Protein, on the other hand, is often regarded only as a means of satiety and for its role in body building. We runners don't exactly gravitate towards the practices of body builders though we appreciate that eating more protein and fewer carbohydrates in our diet can contribute to a leaner physique.

The truth is that protein serves a much more important role in our training diet than bestowing leanness. It is the raw material needed for your muscles to successfully repair themselves. You need it more than you might realize, especially within the first hour or two after a difficult workout. This is the time when your muscles are the most primed for repair and taking advantage of this can ensure optimum delivery of protein to those damaged areas.

Some good protein options following a hard workout:

> *Whey, soy, or another powdered protein mix*
>
> *Eggs*
>
> *Lean meats*
>
> *Milk, yogurt, or another dairy product*
>
> *Nuts*
>
> *Beans*
>
> *Quinoa (this is my favorite plant-based protein source)*

Additionally, following longer distance runs that have also depleted your muscle glycogen, it is also important to take in carbohydrates right after your workout, which will also be primarily directed to your muscles for storage. The concept of nutrient timing is definitely popular in the running world and most books on training nutrition reflect this.

Since we are discussing nutrients for injury prevention and muscle rebuilding, it is important to also mention key micronutrients: vitamins and minerals. Some play larger roles in repairing tissue and preventing injury than others; zinc, for example, has a big role in stimulating cell division and protein synthesis, assembling the raw materials into new muscle tissue.[31] Calcium is an obvious must-take for bone strength, which is particularly important following pregnancy.

Taking a multi-vitamin can ensure that you are getting the spectrum of nutrients that you need, for injury prevention, performance, breastfeeding, everything that you do. The *best* way to get these nutrients, however, is by eating high-quality foods that provide a wide spectrum of vitamins and minerals. Your body is a pretty complex beast and absorbs nutrients best in specific combinations found only in the natural source; cramming them together in a pill doesn't quite work the same way, but is certainly better than not getting enough. Do what works best for you – just make sure you're getting all the goods!

Injury treatments

When injury, unfortunately, arises, we have many options to turn to for treatment. Some practitioners are skilled in multiple types of treatments, and it appears that more and more sports doctors are becoming well-rounded in this way. That is good news for you, in terms of connecting with a local doctor that suits your needs.

Some of the more popular treatments and how they work:

Chiropractor
Chiropractors treat the spine for proper alignment and muscular support. They will ensure that your spinal nerves are not inhibited,

---

[31] For an interesting breakdown of nutrients and athletic activities: www.precisionnutrition.com/

and so signal delivery to and from your lower body muscles (in particular) is optimized. Poor muscle strength and weaknesses in your back can cause problems all the way down your lower body and chiropractors treat this issue starting with the alignment of the spine itself, often with tools that specifically make targeted adjustments. Most sports doctors who specialize in some of the other treatments listed below (A.R.T and Integrative Diagnosis) are trained, first, as chiropractors.

Orthopedics

Orthopedic surgeons treat basically all types of injuries affecting the musculoskeletal system. They have a wide range of specialties and tend to be the go-to source for sports injuries. They are very ubiquitous and easy to find, and some also specialize in the other treatments listed below.

Massage Therapy

A pretty obvious one, massage therapy works to relax and loosen soft tissues specifically relating to your activity. It is not considered a "fix" for injuries but is an effective side-treatment during a rest or recovery period. It can work to break up scar tissue at the site of your injury, which can also expedite healing. Plus, it feels pretty darn good.

Active Release Technique (A.R.T)

This technique has grown in popularity over recent years, especially among highly-competitive runners and triathletes. Practitioners of A.R.T release scar tissue from affected muscles, ligaments, and fascia by directing pressure on affected areas. Like massage, but more targeted. An affected muscle will be taken through its range of motion while pressure is applied, which can be an intense process! There is no one protocol that fits every athlete or situation; practitioners take time to identify which tissues are affected and how they need to be moved or manipulated to function more optimally.[32]

---

[32] A list of A.R.T providers can be found here: www.activerelease.com

Manual Adhesion Release / Instrument Adhesion Release

The objectives of Manual Adhesion Release (M.A.R) and Instrument Adhesion Release (I.A.R) are similar to A.R.T, but with different applications. Both of these techniques are applied as part of an Integrative Diagnosis system, which identifies the source of injury based on function rather than symptoms. A practitioner has the patient go through a series of exercises and movements to assess where the dysfunction is actually located, which is often *not* the site of the pain or discomfort. As they are named, M.A.R is conducted by hand and I.A.R is conducted with a small, flat instrument. To the patient, the application of the therapy seems to be the same as A.R.T, but the diagnosis process is quite different.[33]

Cross training for the win

Last but most definitely not least: for high-performing runners, cross training is critical to injury prevention. This can be accomplished with a very wide variety of activities, from weight room routines to kayaking to biking, and beyond. The value of cross training in injury prevention has been increasingly emphasized by coaches and elite athletes for several key reasons:

> *Resting your running parts, but still getting cardiovascular work done*
>
> *Strengthening your entire muscular system*
>
> *Diversifying your activities for more fun in your routine*

Some activities are better suited for runners than others. I used to do karate as cross training, which was excellent for my muscle strength, cardiovascular strength, and general feeling of badassery. With respect to my flexibility, though, running had an antagonistic relationship with karate; the muscles that become more lengthy and flexible to achieve high kicks and the splits are shortened and tensed by running.

In general, you want your cross training activity to compliment your running, and not duplicate your running form and function *too* much; this

---

[33] My interview with Dr. Maggio at the end of this chapter highlights some of the Integrative Diagnosis philosophy, and he provides a link to find a provider.

means lower impact. The types of activities that most runners engage in include:

Swimming

Biking

Weight-lifting

Elliptical or ElliptiGO

Yoga or Pilates

Cross Fit or Kettlebell classes

Dancing / Zumba

There is certainly a wide range of other things to do too! If you live by big waves, surfing would be an amazing form of balance and stability training. If you live in the mountains, rock climbing can be a great way to build full-body strength.

Strength development is an important part of this, and cannot necessarily be achieved in all forms of cross training. Yoga, for example, is a wonderful complimentary exercise to running in so many ways, but likely does not develop your muscles and tendons adequately for the intensity and high-impact you experience as a highly competitive runner. In that case, you may need to add in some weight lifting.

One of the biggest problems running mamas face is finding the time to work out. As it is, you are probably squeaking out some time to get your running in, let alone additional training. Cross training is not something you need to do as frequently as you run; depending on what it is, you might do it two or three times a week, and it may only last 30 minutes to an hour. For the purposes of strengthening your running body to prevent injury, it is critical that you *do* fit in some cross training throughout your week.

There are creative ways of doing this; yoga on Netflix, body weight strength training at home before bed, and taking baby along in a seat or trailer on your bike are all ways of fitting it in among other activities. When I was recovering from injury, I frequently put Jack in a baby float and pushed him back and forth across the pool; aqua-jogging is a wonderful way to work on your form with minimum impact.

Whatever the way, however, you find a way, it is very important that you fit some cross training into your schedule, especially if you are coming back from an injury! In Chapter 15, we will focus on strength training and its importance in keeping you healthy – during pregnancy, post-pregnancy, and for the long haul.

Ask a Doc: Q & A with Dr. Matt Maggio

It would be remiss of me to not include the perspective of the doctor who literally "saved my butt" when I was battling postpartum injury.

Dr. Matt Maggio is a board-certified chiropractic physician who specializes in Integrative Diagnosis, the application of which are Manual & Instrument Adhesion techniques. I sought out his practice, Peak Performance Sports Therapy LLC, here in St. Petersburg at the recommendation of some fellow runners. His philosophy emphasizes targeted treatment of soft tissue injuries by identifying the sources of functional weaknesses, rather than just treating the symptoms.

Though the treatment of my hip and glute problems required more rest time than I wanted at the time (but really not long at all, in the scope of things), I trusted his judgement and the methods he employs, and came out far stronger than I had imagined possible. I remember during some of my first comeback runs feeling as if someone was literally pushing my hamstrings up and forward. My stride and hip extension was light-years ahead of where it had been. He treated dysfunction that I didn't know existed, which was the first step on my own journey of building a stronger running body. PR's followed, and I still check in with Dr. Maggio every so often for a "tune up" look at my form and range of motion.

When I told him about writing this book, he enthusiastically agreed to contribute some of his experiences and advice. My questions and his responses:

Q: What are the most common injuries you see among female athletes following pregnancy?

A: The majority of what I see tends to be in the low back area. In my opinion, the increased amount of ligament laxity coupled with the weight gain can put a lot of added stress onto the low back musculature. Especially in the muscles that stabilize the lumbar spine. A majority of women do suffer some low back pain at some point during their pregnancy. The issue that comes after the delivery is the accumulation of scar tissue that has become present from the muscles being in a state of constant contraction. In most "normal" mothers who just exercise recreationally this really doesn't cause more than an occasional twinge. In female athletes who need full capacity of the muscles to do the activity the scar tissue formation becomes more of a problem and pushes them over symptom threshold.

Q: When a woman's hips widen during pregnancy and childbirth, what kind of long-term effects does that have on her lower body musculature? Do these effects pose injury risks?

A: I think in terms of simple evolution and the biology of pregnancy, this shouldn't pose any problem, but that isn't the case in our modern society. We end up sitting far too much, which ends up putting more stress on the hips during the whole pregnancy. The hips and musculature of the lower body are meant to be upright and moving, even when pregnant, but that doesn't happen today as we live in a society where we sit too much. I think this becomes an issue for the ligaments of the hips and surrounding musculature of being overloaded too much from sitting, but also can cause them to be deconditioned quicker than we think.

Q: How do hormonal changes in a pregnant and/or breastfeeding mother affect her athletic activities?

A: _Prolactin_ and _relaxin_ can cause a lot of issues with the mother that wants to maintain her "competitive edge". Having a baby and breastfeeding is a huge stressor on the body. The number one priority is to keep the infant healthy, often at the expense of the mother's own health. This becomes an issue similar to the one addressed above, except in the opposite way. Many competitive mothers want to get back into activity as quickly as possible and often train too hard for too long into the pregnancy. The body is preparing for a traumatic event – birth - and piling on a lot of extra "stress" of a demanding physical regiment can be detrimental. The needs of the baby will always take precedent, so training too hard will have a negative consequence on the mother's body.

Q: It appears that many female athletes – especially elites – return to their running stronger and faster in the year or two after having a baby. Do you agree? If so, what do you think can be attributed to their success?

A: I completely agree with this notion. I polled a few other doctors as well on this and we all agreed on what it can be attributed to: rest! Most elite runners and athletes are training at a level of diminished capacity, which is always putting them in a hole as far as recovery. Never reaching back to normal baseline from proper recovery leads to functioning at a limited capacity, never reaching their full potential. Having an infant that takes up a majority of the mother's time has a way of almost forcing the mother into getting rest. When proper rest is achieved, it allows the body to function at full capacity, thus leading to a stronger and faster body. Most people over-train and never realize they are missing out on the full potential they have, only focusing on quantity, not quality.

Q: From your perspective and expertise, do you have any advice for pregnant or postpartum competitive runners on retaining their training gains, continuing to compete, and avoiding injury?

A: This is a great question and I could go on forever with this, but I will hit the key points.

Listen to your body. Pain or symptoms are the body trying to tell you that something is going wrong. Ignoring symptoms over a long term will always lead to an injury.

Rest, rest and then rest some more. Give your body time to recover. If you are always going 100 percent, you will always be digging a hole as far as recovery. I say it to patients all the time: train smarter, not harder!

Practice varied activities. A majority of injuries come from repetitive overuse, doing the same movements every day. Have a variety of movement. Don't just do one thing all the time. Sprinkle in some variety! This will keep you from developing repetitive strain injuries.

Do some self-maintenance on your body. Foam rolling, mobility work, and stretching are good for pumping blood through the muscles. It also serves as an early warning if something is going wrong or just doesn't feel quite right. These are great when you aren't injured, similar to brushing your teeth every day.

Bring in a professional. Go get a massage. They are great for relaxing and helping you recover. Take a yoga class or try acupuncture. They are all a great way to help your body feel good.

Finally, if you are injured, then get an assessment! Some of the best doctors in the world are trained in the Integrative Diagnosis system. This system focuses on restoring muscle capacity and fixing biomechanics. You can go here to see if you have one in your area:

http://www.integrativediagnosis.com/Pages/FindProvider.aspx

Chapter 15
Get Strong

I live in Florida. The Sunshine State. Known for a variety of intriguing and entertaining attributes, one of which only seems to come up during particularly intense summer and fall seasons: hurricanes. While we don't experience severe hurricanes very often, we are extremely susceptible to death and devastation when they do happen, as is the rest of the Gulf Coast.

One of the things that has always bothered me about our great state is the prevalence of weak, poorly-constructed buildings. During the intense and unprecedented 2004 hurricane season, a college friend and I were watching the news coverage of Hurricane Charley's landfall, virtually obliterating much of the towns of Punta Gorda and Port Charlotte. There were images of houses from across the spectrum of "class", from fancy new construction to older wooden houses to modular homes, all reduced to nothing but flattened, scattered sticks sprawled across the county. What used to be parks, beaches, and waterfront neighborhoods were completely submerged in water. My friend watching with me was from Jamaica, and I asked him if his neighborhoods at home ever look this bad after a hurricane, since Jamaica gets far more frequently pummeled by tropical storms than we do. He shook his head, knocked on the drywall next to him, and said "See this? We don't ever build with this crap. Everywhere is mostly brick construction."

What relevance does this story have to strength training?

We should build our bodies for running the same way Jamaicans build their homes for hurricanes: by acknowledging the likelihood of damage. When you are risking probable, eventual damage – as our running bodies are, and as buildings in the tropics are - you must build your structures to be as sturdy as possible. No skimping on structural integrity; rebuilding what was broken is far more devastating than the work necessary to be prepared.

Consistent, routine strength training is the most effective way of ensuring that you have a strong, "hurricane-ready" runner body. This concept is often disregarded by many runners, especially female runners, for a variety of reasons:

I don't have time to strength train.

Running makes me strong enough by itself.

I don't want to get big and bulky.

I seem to be doing just fine without it

Mamas, it is long past time to deconstruct some persistent myths surrounding strength training, and make sure we get to the gym. Or the living room floor. Or wherever you can train. Because strength training is the single greatest tool for achieving two critical components of your running life: injury prevention and faster race times.

You can also involve your family in this aspect of training. I even have some exercises you can do with baby. Seems kind of cliché, I know, but you'll seriously have many days where your little one insists on being a part of *everything*. It sure allows you to kill many birds with fewer stones. Metaphorically, of course.

Weight, weight, don't tell me

Turning to the weight room is one of the more popular and accessible options for runners to implement strength training into their routine. Gyms can be found nearly anywhere and there are countless different ways to mix-up a weight routine. Many gyms also have some pretty awesome fitness classes to choose from, which can provide great cross training option.

While coaching girls in track and cross country, one of the most common and persistent misconceptions I had to break is that weight training will make them big and bulky. They imagine pictures of female body builders with large, veiny muscles and balk at how unfeminine this appears to them (we can debate *that* issue on another day).

What they don't realize is how very, very difficult it is for female body builders to achieve that physique. It requires a strict diet that cannot support endurance activities, very little cardiovascular exercise, and a far more directed regimen of weight lifting than is necessary for runners. Even if you tried to bulk up, *you simply can't do it with the amount of running you are also doing.*

Running and bodybuilding are opposing and counteractive processes in terms of the physical composition of your body. Like other highly cardiovascular activities, running is <u>catabolic</u>, meaning that your metabolism is breaking down larger structures (including muscle tissue) into smaller molecules and releasing energy used to power yourself along. Recovery and weight lifting are <u>anabolic</u> activities, meaning that smaller molecules are used to build larger structures. Running breaks things down, lifting builds things up. This is why professional bodybuilders only do only a small amount of cardio to burn calories and "trim away fat", but otherwise avoid cardio altogether.

This is also why recovery and strength training are so crucial to injury prevention and speed development in your running. If you are running daily but not taking time to rest or strength train, you are essentially breaking down your body without re-building it and expecting it to keep working well.

In the first couple of postpartum years, your body has already experienced a serious strain and needs to re-strengthen before it performs as well as it did pre-pregnancy. A balanced, comprehensive approach to weight lifting provides this refortification, improves your running form, and greatly reduces the chance of future injuries.

Bad tone

I can't count the number of times I have overheard a girl or woman say the following:

"I don't want to build muscle, I just want to get toned."

The implication of this statement is that building muscle makes you appear bulky, an undesirable outcome, and getting 'toned' equates to a svelte, feminine appearance.

Let's be clear about what "getting toned" actually means. The popular use of the term "muscle tone" refers to the visible definition of muscle on a person. Such a person is lean and their muscles are firm and well-defined. The actual physiological definition of "muscle tone" is different, referring to the subconsciously-contracted state of muscles such that they are firm, not flaccid while you are at rest.[34] In the interest of this discussion, I will refer to "getting toned" in the popular sense: visibly defined muscles.

How does one achieve this tone? Two ways, or ideally a combination of both: building muscle and reducing body fat. Since fat covers muscles, reducing body fat will itself make someone appear more "toned" by exposing more muscles just below the skin. Otherwise, one must increase their muscle mass in order to appear "toned". So the idea of lifting weights to get toned without building muscle is kind of an oxymoron.

Either way that you do it, approaching strength training with the goal of only "getting toned" is problematic. Such a goal is about appearance, not about actual strength. Serious runners need to be more concerned with their body's functionality than its appearance, and the mistaken notion that one needs to limit their heavy weight lifting or strength development least they "get bulky" is detrimental to healthy training.

Funny thing is that the desired svelte, "toned" appearance is more likely achieved through running and *heavy* weight lifting than through just running or adding in only light lifting. Which brings us to our next myth in need of busting...

How heavy & how many
Another fairly persistent myth in weight lifting is that doing lighter weights at high repetitions is more effective at fat burning and getting "toned" than doing heavier weights at fewer repetitions. Maybe it's because doing more reps can also be a cardiovascular process, especially when done quickly and with little rest in between sets (but if that's the case, why not just do cardio for fat burning?) Maybe it's because many women associate lifting larger weights with, well, getting larger.

Whatever the reason, strength training with only low weights at high reps does *not* burn more fat than heavier weights at lower reps. On the

---

[34] The fitness site, ShapeSense.com, provides several articles with great perspective on the differences in muscle definition.

contrary, using heavier weights stimulates a different physiological response than lower weights, and is actually involved in releasing hormones that trigger fat utilization during and after the workout.[35]

More importantly for you, engaging in *only* low-weight/high-rep workouts won't be effective in reaching your goals of developing speed, improving strength, and avoiding injury.

It's all about muscle fibers, just like running sprints versus running long distance. Low-weight/high-rep weight lifting will recruit more slow-twitch muscle fibers for endurance, and high-weight/low rep lifting will recruit more fast-twitch, explosive muscle fibers. As a runner, you benefit from both of these, but with all the running you are putting in, you really don't need to spend much gym time developing the former.

That having been said if you are not running due to injury or pregnancy, but can otherwise engage in weight lifting, mixing in some low-weight/high-rep workouts can help you retain some endurance.

Developing explosive muscle power will contribute significantly to your speed, whether your race is the mile or the marathon. This is one of the biggest components of competitive racing that we can all improve upon, and the thing that tends to decline the most with age. High-weight/low-rep training will improve your speed, especially when applied as part of a consistent, methodical strength program.

Getting with the program

While I don't include specific strength training programs in this book, I do want to provide some general guidelines and tips for successfully implementing a strength program into your routine, both during and after pregnancy (see the next section for some example exercises and demonstrations that can be done with baby). There are many resources out there to help you find them, and even better, learn how to develop them for yourself, some of which I provide in the Resources section.

---

[35] Most body building and weight training websites have great resources illustrating the differences in types of muscle fibers and the physiological reactions to different exercises, the most comprehensive of which is: www.bodybuilding.com. Don't shy away from body building resources, even if you have no intention of "body building"!

In developing a weight lifting program, you want it to achieve the following:

> 1. Work a multitude of muscle groups, especially those most prone to running-related injuries
>
> 2. Work in cycles: several weeks of a starting point and slowly increasing in weight and adjusting number of reps as necessary
>
> 3. Be done routinely. Most running wisdom says 2-3 times per week is sufficient to make major improvements
>
> 4. Compliment your running schedule (for example, no weight lifting the morning before a tough running workout, or the week of a significant race).
>
> 5. Allow for rest and recovery with at least a day in between.

This might sound like an impossible task: routine, but with a day's rest in between, and not right before a running workout. It is tricky, and may take some time to nail down, but can be achieved. Maybe do a gym day on your day(s) off from running. Or maybe even do your strength workout right after a run, if you have child care covered during that time. Trial and error will yield the system that works best for you. Many gyms have a child care service; you can drop your little one off for some play time with other kids and new toys while you are working out just on the other side of the building. Additionally, having access to a gym can definitely be helpful with respect to the variety and types of equipment available to you.

Below are some general recommendations for selecting strength exercises.

> **Multi-task**
> Choose exercises that work multiple muscles at once, rather than just one or two. This is more efficient, and thus easier on your schedule! These would include lunges with weights, plyometrics, stability ball crunches and curls, and power cleans. Not only are they more efficient, they are dynamic, which forces your entire body to work a little bit harder to stabilize itself.

The core of the matter
Core training is critical for runners though frequently goes misunderstood. Most people work their abdominal muscles since those provide that lovely six pack. Your abs are part of your core, but they are not the whole package. Back, hip and gluteal muscles are also part of your core. These muscles stabilize your body during every stage of your running stride, and the hip and glutes provide the power behind it. Do not neglect them! Choose exercises that emphasize these critical areas.

Help your hammys
Runners are mostly quadricep-dominant. This means that your quads, the large, powerful muscles on the front of your femur, are much stronger than your hamstrings. This disparity between the two can lead to problems in running form and the strain placed upon the hips in stabilizing your lower body. It is very important to balance the workload between your quads and hamstrings, especially following pregnancy. Maybe avoid the leg press in favor of hammy-specific exercises for a while to ensure that they are developing proportionally.

Power upper
It is not uncommon for runners to neglect working out their upper body. After all, you don't use your upper body when you run, right? *WRONG.* Your arm swings drive your lower body. Your shoulder and deltoid muscles stabilize the upper part of your spine. Having a strong upper body is just as important for runners as it is for many other types of athletes. Thankfully, you are constantly getting a good amount of upper body strength just by taking care of a little bundle that is perpetually increasing in weight. Carrying your little one around will make a noticeable difference in your arm strength! All the same, it is still important not to neglect your upper body in your strength routine

If you have the option of strength training at home, you have a lot more flexibility in terms of time and logistics. Maybe you own machines or free weights, and maybe you only have a few other exercise supplies; either way, you can generally get some excellent strength work done with some basics. Though achieving the higher weight / lower rep types of workouts can be a little trickier without a complete set of free weights or machines, your own body weight can be a great tool for this. Some excellent body weight exercises include:

Push-ups, of all kind and variety

Wall-sits

Squats, holding baby or other heavy objects

Lunges, holding baby or other heavy objects

Chin-ups or pull-ups, if you have a bar with which to do this

Planks, of all kind and variety

Triceps dip, using a chair or sofa

There are countless ways that you can get good strength training done: in a gym, at home, at a cross fit or boot camp class. However you do it, the important thing is to *make your strength training a priority*. Be just as irritated when you miss a day of strength training as you are when you miss a run. Your strength training keeps you running healthy! Protect it, and you protect your running.

Working out with baby

While you are on maternity leave and beyond, you are spending a great deal of time with baby. Most of this time is definitely accounted for: feeding, soothing, changing diapers, bathing, playing, tickling, laughing, strolling, and so on. When you need to get some strength training in, baby provides an excellent opportunity for both of you. You have this little free weight that is getting heavier every day who is much more fun to lift than a gym weight. Do kettlebells giggle and smile at you? I think not.

Incorporating baby into your strength training can be great fun for both of you. You can now strength train virtually anywhere and spend quality time with your little one in the process. I have some examples of good exercises with baby (Figures 18-20), but there are certainly more ways of doing these. Many "mommy and me" workout groups do these, too.

Some important notes about working out with baby:

If baby is still very young, make sure his/her head is well supported.

Be sensitive to where you put pressure on baby when you hold him/her away from your body.

Keep your <u>back straight</u> and <u>lift with your legs</u>! Even if baby is still quite small and light.

Proceed with caution if baby just ate...

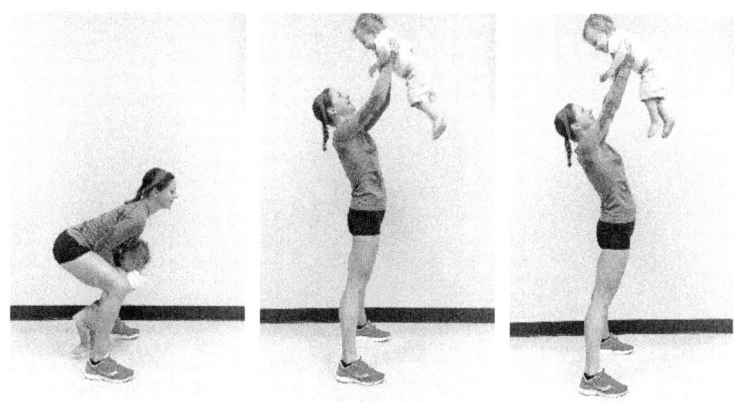

Figure 14 – Baby thrust: like kettle bells, but with smiles! Keep your back straight and lift from the legs, engaging your hamstrings.

Figure 15 – Baby thrust: generally the same exercise as in Figure 17, but with baby facing forward. This may allow a little more "swing" during the squat phase, and likely result in more giggles.

Figure *16* – Baby lunge: can also be done by switching baby side to side, if he/she enjoys it. Keep your back straight and push off from the heels.

Figure *17* – Baby sit-up: there are many ways of doing this one. Best achieved with kiss at the top.

Mighty Mama: Nancy Smith

Age: 43

Home: St Petersburg, FL

Profession: Professor of Marine Science at Eckerd College

Children: Daughter, Nya, 6 years old.

When I was 13 years old, I witnessed one of the most exciting running events – an event that inspired me to become a long-distance runner and join the women's cross-country team when I started high school. This incredible day taught me that women can do and achieve anything men could do, and the stereotypes that running was bad for women's health (which was common place in the 1970's when I was growing up), particularly reproductive health, quickly dissipated that day.

On May 12, 1984, the first women's U.S. Olympic Trials Marathon was held in my hometown of Olympia, Washington. I sat near mile-marker 25 and watched every female runner go by. Joan Benoit, the fastest women I've ever seen, won the race that day (she went on to win the first Olympic women's marathon in Los Angeles that summer!) Equally amazing was watching a very pregnant women (6 months pregnant!) complete the marathon. She was in last place, but when she went by, every spectator stood up and cheered her on. This was so amazing to me because I've never seen a pregnant woman run or compete before, and I didn't know that it was possible to do so. This memory is important to me because when I became pregnant with Nya, I had no doubt that I could continue to run during my pregnancy. I think back to that day a lot because it was the day that I committed myself to the sport.

As a side note - When I was growing up (born in 1971 and went to high school in the mid to late 80's), it was rare to see women compete in long-distance running events. In fact, women's long distance running was a very young sport, and my coach even had trouble getting enough girls for our cross-country team (which only consisted of 2-3 women in any given season). I think one of the greatest accomplishments in women's running over the past 20-30 years has been the growth, in both numbers and acceptance of the sport. When I compete in today's races, at least half of the competitors are women. It's been amazing to see this positive change in my own lifetime - and I'm not that old!

In the Vietnamese culture (I'm half-Vietnamese), the conventional wisdom is that running is bad for women, also a common stereotype in American culture in the 1960's and 1970's. Some members in my family still believe that women can lose their femininity if they run regularly. When I share photos of me running, my family remind me that running is not good for me or my health, and I should consider stopping. When I was pregnant with Nya, I didn't want to tell anyone, including my mom, that I was continuing my runs during the pregnancy. I can only imagine what they would say.

During my pregnancy, I asked my doctor if it was safe for me to run and I was told that I could continue whatever distance and level that I was doing as long as I was doing it before the pregnancy. So, I continued my normal routine which consisted of three days of running with distances varying from 4 to 10 miles, and I did yoga between running days. I decreased my weekly mileage from approximately 30-35 miles down to 20 miles when I was pregnant. By the time April-May hit, it was getting too hot and humid to run; I was 5-6 months pregnant and I was getting dehydrated more easily. I stopped running by the third trimester and turned to swimming, which was the perfect activity during the hot summer. I had Nya in late July 2009, and I was 38 years old.

After Nya was born, it took me 3-4 months to get back to exercising. Honestly, the first three months was such a blur that I don't remember much except that I barely slept and I stayed in the house on most days. After having the fall semester off, I came back to Eckerd full-time (teaching, research, mentoring) and it was very hard since I was still breastfeeding Nya. At this time, my exercise routine mainly consisted of running on weekends, and doing yoga during the week to deal with the stress of a new baby and a demanding job. By the time Nya was one year old, I had returned to running three days a week, building back up to about 30 miles per week. I experienced my first injury several months later, my only running injury since high school, 20 years earlier!

For the first time, I had developed shin splints. The pain became progressively worse and because I never got a bone scan or MRI (which I should have done, in retrospect), it's quite possible that my shin splint developed into a tibial stress fracture since the pain become more localized and got worse during long runs. When walking began to hurt, I had no choice but to stop running for a few months and let the bone heal. After my recovery, I went back to running (slowly!) and started to train for the local half marathons.

After doing three half marathons about a year after my shin splint first developed, I got plantar fasciitis, which got progressively worse as I ran distances longer than about fifteen miles. I took a few months off to heal the foot completely because it was causing me to limp and the injury was becoming chronic. By this time Nya was 3 years old. I was really frustrated with the injuries and knew that I had to change my approach.

I read lots of articles about how strength training could reduce knee, leg and foot pain/injuries, so I decided to join the YMCA to use their equipment and take strength training classes, such as Les Mills Body Pump. After taking the classes for several months at the Y, I decided to take my fitness to a higher level, so I hired a personal trainer. My goal was to run faster, stronger, and injury-free. I've been working with Eddie – my personal trainer, power lifter, tabata instructor – 2 days per week for almost 2 years and the cross training has helped me achieve those goals. The sessions consisted of body building exercises with free-weights and barbells, and using heavy weights for squats, bench presses, deadlifts, etc. I believe that this type of training has helped me become faster and able to run longer distances without pain or injuries.

Of course, I'll never be able to run a 5:40 mile like I did in high school track, but I'm still pretty competitive compared to other women in their mid-40's. I only wish I started the strength training earlier as it could have prevented or reduced the injuries, and recover more effectively from the disruption of the pregnancy.

I am currently recovering from a femoral stress fracture (this time I got an MRI and didn't self-diagnose) which is probably the result of too much racing/speed work and switching to minimalist shoes. Aging is probably another contributing factor. The type of stress fracture that I have is really rare; it's in the distal part of the femur near the knee joint, and is only found in women who run long-distances, have a lead body mass, are over the age of 40, and have a Caucasian or Asian background (bone turn-over and mineralization rates tend to be lower in women have these traits).

I think my comeback will be stronger because my fitness is at a higher level and I've been doing more active recovery and preventative measures than before. So, I've had three major injuries in the past five years and I'm sure that injuries will continue as I get older, and as I keep racing and running. But it's still worth it.

Chapter 16
The Long Road Ahead

The world of women's running is an incredible, awe-inspiring force that just grows in positive power. Kathrine Switzer's presence in the '67 Boston Marathon ignited an uproar over the issue of *whether or not women should be allowed to run marathons,* and here I am, just under fifty years later, writing a book about competitive running and pregnancy, because there are so, so many of us serious running mamas out there. I smile at the thought of where women's running will go in the next fifty years.

You've got an incredible running life ahead of you, mama. Only time knows where, exactly, it will take you. There are so many tools and resources at your disposal to ensure that it is fast, fulfilling, and successful, however you choose to define it. Best of all, you have a wonderful child (or many) with whom to share this empowering part of your life.

As we've discussed in previous chapters, you have the potential and capacity to continue improving your running for many years to come, *especially* after pregnancy, and even as age sneakily starts to affect your athletic abilities. It is important, though, to keep your sights set on new challenges and opportunities as they present themselves.

Going the distance

The goals you set for yourself as a runner are fluid. They may change as you re-discover yourself as a runner, either post-baby or post-surgery or post-anything else that has the potential to change your body. In all likelihood, you will achieve them, and then want to develop new goals. For many runners, this becomes a new distance.

Ultramarathon running is not nearly as common among younger (twenty-something) age runners as it is among older runners.[36] This is partially due

---

[36] In a study on the demographics and behavior of 1,345 ultra-runners, the average age of first-time ultra-runners was 36 years old, and 25% of ultra-runners

to the accumulated fitness and mental discipline necessary to succeed at distances beyond the marathon, and the fact that the raw speed necessary to be competitive at shorter distances tends to be harder to sustain as you get older. In any case, running an ultra is a common and wonderful future goal. There is a growing community of longer-distance runners and increasing opportunities to race at ultramarathon distances. Maybe you are already an ultra-runner and are pursuing different distances, race locations, or challenges within the category of longer-than-26.2 races. More and more racing options are arising as the sport grows in popularity.

Just TRI it

Becoming a triathlete is perhaps the most popular way of diversifying your competitive fitness. Perhaps you swim or bike as cross training, though running is your main competitive focus, and taking the next step to competing in a triathlon is the natural next step. This is also a sport that has grown considerably in recent years and features a very broad spectrum of distances.

Best of all about triathlons: you run a lessened risk of running-specific injuries if you divide your endurance training across swimming and cycling as well. This makes triathlons appealing to runners who have battled injuries or are simply ready to change-up their competitive lifestyle. Is it more expensive than just running? Yes, it is, there is no way around that. But there are lots of ways to acquire tri-specific gear – bike, wetsuit, clothing, etc. – that make the sport perfectly attainable.

Happy trails

If you have spent most of your running life on roads, consider hitting the trails for some of your training and setting some trail-racing goals. Trails are fun, trails are scenic, and trail running can really strengthen tendons and ligaments in your lower body, making you a stronger runner in general. The softer impact of running on dirt, as opposed to roads or sidewalks, will also benefit your knees and shins, both body parts that have the potential to suffer after many years of pounding pavement.

---

had only been running consistently for 3 year prior to their first!

Seeking adventure

Also booming in popularity over the past few years are adventure races. These are the races that take you through mud, over obstacles, under barb wire, through fire, and basically every other malady you can imagine. They are boot-camp inspired challenges that certainly utilize your running ability, but also your body strength and grit.

These races may not appear to be the province of "serious runners", but instead that of the everyday-person who wants to challenge themselves to accomplish a tough, muddy, badass kind of obstacle. Road 5Ks have a similar appeal and it doesn't diminish the seriousness of 5K racing to competitive or elite runners. Adventure races certainly do have serious, high-level competitors who have much more than just running speed and endurance; these guys and gals are *fierce*, ripped, and skilled at hand-eye type tasks that most running purists would shudder at the thought of attempting. Make no mistake, adventure racing poses plenty of new and diverse challenges.

Share the love

In reflecting on the best elements of my running life, I was somewhat surprised to find that most of my favorite running-related memories were coaching memories. Sure, my most recent marathon PR and the first time I qualified for Boston pop into my mind. But right up there with them are visions of seeing the young men and women I coached powering up a tough hill in a race, screaming cheers for a teammate crossing the finish line, that extra jump in their stride when they realize they are about to set a PR, coming back from their run covered in mud and grinning ear to ear, sweaty group hugs at the end of the championship meet, and the funny, nervous antics they would act out while waiting for their race to start.

Many seasoned runners decide to become personal coaches, advertising primarily to adults. Others, like myself, get hired at a school to coach a middle school or high school competitive track or cross country team. If you're part of a local running club, you can work your way into the ranks of coaching your peers. Online coaching is now a growing enterprise, where in coaches develop training plans and frequently communicate with their trainees via social networking, email, phone, or text.

Coaching brings out a new part of yourself, and with it you are helping others achieve their dreams. If you love running, coaching can be sheer joy. Sharing your passion with those who want to improve their running, whether they are 10 years old or 70 years old, can enrich your own running life in ways that you may not expect. It can really happen anyway that you want it to. It isn't for everyone, but I highly recommend considering it as your running career develops.

Life lessons

The fall racing season is always my favorite, coming out of the intensity of Florida summers and banking on heat training fitness. Last year, when I was finally healthy and back to racing again, every weekend was either one of my stepson's cross country meets or one of my races. His meets were usually in the afternoon, but my morning races required early rising on a Saturday or Sunday.

I remember feeling badly for my stepson; he was a busy teenager who was tired from his own training and waking early on the weekend to watch me race. I let him off the hook at some point, telling him that he didn't have to come to my race if he didn't want to, that if he needed some sleep-in time it was OK. My feelings would not be hurt. He took me up on this just once, for one race. But the next time I raced, he was up with the alarm clock and ready to go. He wanted to support my running. At the end of his track season that year, he told me that he wanted to get faster and asked me to help him. I hadn't realized until then how the example I was setting in my training and discipline had influenced him. From the races we ran together to my most recent PR-setting marathon, my running was inspiring him.

I think we have all experienced something like this. When you actually realize the power you have to set a positive example for your kids, and that the life lessons they can gain from your actions are not even intentional, the sense of responsibility can suddenly be overwhelming.

An unfortunate notion that seems to permeate the modern parenting paradigm is that once you become a parent, *every single thing* you do must be *all* about your kids. That if you're putting considerable time and energy into something for yourself, you are selfish and a lesser parent. I say this is "unfortunate" because I believe this notion to be neither a healthy mindset for parents, nor an effective strategy at raising strong, secure, independent children. My further commentary on this subject are for another time, place, or book; I only mention it to make one point particularly clear: *your running life is extremely positive for your kids, precisely <u>because</u> you create it for yourself, not in spite of the fact.*

As runners, we have a wonderful, important opportunity to be incredible role models for our kids.

We show them the necessity of hard work and discipline.

The importance of perseverance.

The effectiveness of patience.

The introspection that comes from spending time in their own heads.

The beauty of teamwork.

The importance of good sleep.

The importance of a healthy diet.

The thrill of competition.

That talent alone won't fulfill their potential.

That their bodies are beautiful, amazing tools for chasing their dreams.

How to handle losing with grace.

How to handle winning with grace.

How to trust their training.

How to believe in their strength.

How to think positively, even when the outlook is grim.

The list could go on, and on.

Your children get to see you as a runner in addition to being "mom". Maybe they do consistently observe you in other capacities as well if you coach their soccer team or teach at their school. In any case, they witness you accomplishing things that don't revolve around *their* needs. They become more outwardly-focused, capable young people when they understand that their parents are, indeed, also people, with goals and dreams and successful methods of reaching them. They need to see you as more than just some altruistic being that exists for *their* needs.

You need to see yourself this way, first and foremost. Having a baby significantly changes your life, and you are now a stronger runner because of it. Let running continue to be the fire that ignites your spirit, keeps you sane, powers your successes, heals your failures, and inspires your children to learn how to cultivate the same joy in their lives.

Embrace this change. Let life change your running, and running will keep changing your life.

Acknowledgements

I cannot tell you how special this book-writing process has been for me, especially as my own training and mother-runner experiences progressed during the time that I wrote it. It is very much a living document in that sense.

I feel a profound sense of gratitude for the running community that has supported me through this process: friends, acquaintances, and total strangers who provided thoughts, ideas, advice, and moral support when needed. Thank you, all of you!

A BIG shout-out to the incredible Mighty Mamas, who contributed their perspectives. It is an honor to be your storytelling instrument and I am certain that others will be so very inspired by each of you.

Finally, a big thank you to my wonderful husband, Stephen, who never faltered in support and encouragement of this project. I couldn't have done it without him. I wouldn't be a mother without him!

Favorite Resources

Runner's Connect

Training plans, resources, & tools for runners of all levels and abilities. Excellent podcast!

www.runnersconnect.net

Oiselle

Running apparel for women, resources on training and team, wonderful community.

www.oiselle.com

FitPregnancy

Articles, advice, gear, and basically any information you seek on fitness and pregnancy.

www.fitpregnancy.com

Every Mother Counts

Non-profit founded by Christy Turlington Burns, dedicated to providing care and resources for pregnant women worldwide and improving maternal health.

www.everymothercounts.org

Great Blogs & Sites

Ask Lauren Fleshman

www.asklaurenfleshman.com

Kara Goucher

www.karagoucher.com

Ben & Steph Bruce

www.stephandbenbruce.com

Deena Kastor

www.deenakastor.com

Kathrine Switzer – Marathon Woman

www.kathrineswitzer.com

NYC Running Mama – Michelle Gonzales

www.nycrunningmama.com

Run Far Girl – Sarah Canney

www.runfargirl.com

Hungry Runner Girl – Janae Jacobs

www.hungryrunnergirl.com

See Mom Run Far – Erin Henderson

www.seemomrunfar.blogspot.com

Mommy Run Fast – Laura Peifer

www.mommyrunfast.com

The Runner's Plate – Michelle Baxter

www.therunnersplate.com

Florida Road Races

www.FloridaRoadRaces.com

References

AAPM&R - American Academy of Physical Medicine and Rehabilitation. (2015). Retrieved June 27, 2015, from https://www.aapmr.org/patients/conditions/msk/Pages/runfact.aspx

Active Release Techniques. (n.d.). Retrieved July 9, 2015, from http://www.activerelease.com/index.asp

Adrenocorticotropic Hormone. (n.d.). Retrieved July 16, 2015, from http://www.webmd.com/children/adrenocorticotropic-hormone

Aschwanden, C. (2009, January 20). Age Matters. Retrieved June 2, 2015, from http://www.runnersworld.com/masters-training/age-matters

Beilock, S., Feltz, D., & Pivarnik, J. (2001). Training Patterns of Athletes during Pregnancy and Postpartum. *Research Quarterly for Exercise and Sport, 72*(1), 39-46.

Berardi, J. (2013, June 21). Nutrition for Injury Recovery: Part 4 | Precision Nutrition. Retrieved June 2, 2015, from http://www.precisionnutrition.com/nutrition-for-injury-part-4

Bonyata, K. (2014). KellyMom.com : Exercise and Breastfeeding. Retrieved June 3, 2015, from http://kellymom.com/bf/can-i-breastfeed/lifestyle/mom-exercise/

Bouchard, C., & Hoffman, E. (2011). Genetic & Molecular Aspects of Sports Performance. In *Encyclopaedia of Sports Medicine* (1st ed., Vol. 18, pp. 98-370). International Olympic Committee.

Braam, L., Knapen, M., Geusens, P., Brouns, F., & Vermeer, C. (2003). Factors Affecting Bone Loss in Female Endurance Athletes: A Two-Year Follow-Up Study. *American Journal of Sports Medicine, 31*(6), 889-895.

Carpenter, M., Sady, S., Sady, M., Haydon, B., Coustan, D., & Thompson, P. (1990). Effect of maternal weight gain during pregnancy on exercise performance. *Journal of Applied Physiology, 68*(3), 1173-1176.

Cheung, K., Hume, P., & Maxwell, L. (2012). Delayed Onset Muscle Soreness. *Sports Medicine, 33*(2), 145-164.

Clapp, J. (2012). Exercise Effects on Fetoplacental Growth. In *Exercising through your pregnancy* (2nd ed.). Omaha, Nebraska: Addicus Books.

Clapp, J., & Capeless, E. (1991). The VO2max of recreational athletes before and after pregnancy. *Medicine & Science in Sports & Exercise,23*(10), 1128-1133.

Colleran, H., Wideman, L., & Lovelady, C. (1998). Effects of Energy Restriction and Exercise on Bone Mineral Density during Lactation.*Medicine & Science in Sports & Exercise, 128*(2), 1570-1579.

Diastasis Recti: Why Ab Separation Happens and How It's Treated. (2015). Retrieved July 16, 2015, from http://www.webmd.com/baby/guide/abdominal-separation-diastasis-recti

Douglass, S. (2013, May 8). Risk Factors for Injury in New Runners. Retrieved May 4, 2015, from http://www.runnersworld.com/newswire/risk-factors-for-injury-in-new-runners

Dragoo, J., Castillo, T., Braun, H., Ridley, B., Kennedy, A., & Golish, S. (2011). Prospective Correlation Between Serum Relaxin Concentration and Anterior Cruciate Ligament Tears Among Elite Collegiate Female Athletes. *The American Journal of Sports Medicine, 39*(10), 2175-2180. doi:10.1177/0363546511413378

Druxman, L. (2003). The Pregnant Athlete. Retrieved August 2, 2015, from http://www.ideafit.com/fitness-library/the-pregnant-athlete

Dunn, J., Dunn, C., Habbu, R., Bohay, D., & Anderson, J. (2012). Effect of Pregnancy and Obesity on Arch of Foot. *Orthopaedic Surgery, 4*(2), 101-104. doi:10.1111/j.1757-7861.2012.00179.x

Fat Loss & Weight Training Myths. (n.d.). Retrieved July 16, 2015, from http://www.exrx.net/WeightTraining/Myths.html

Foods to Avoid During Pregnancy. (2012, April 26). Retrieved May 14, 2015, from http://americanpregnancy.org/pregnancy-health/foods-to-avoid-during-pregnancy/

Foran, J. (2013). Transient Osteoporosis of the Hip-OrthoInfo - AAOS. Retrieved July 2, 2015, from http://orthoinfo.aaos.org/topic.cfm?topic=A00205

Gilleard, W. (2013). Trunk motion and gait characteristics of pregnant women when walking: Report of a longitudinal study with a control group. *BMC Pregnancy Childbirth, 13*, 71-71. doi:10.1186/1471-2393-13-71.

HON Mother & Child Glossary, Cardiovascular System Changes during Pregnancy. (2002, June 25). Retrieved July 10, 2015, from https://www.hon.ch/Dossier/MotherChild/preg_changes/circulation.html

Hochwald, L. (2011). A Cheat Sheet to Pregnancy Hormones. Retrieved June 6, 2015, from http://www.parents.com/pregnancy/my-life/emotions/understanding-pregnancy-hormones/

Hoffman, M., & Krishnan, E. (2013). Exercise Behavior of Ultramarathon Runners. *Journal of Strength and Conditioning Research, 27*(11), 2939-2945. doi:10.1519/JSC.0b013e3182a1f261

How much does age effect running performance - is it all downhill after 40? (2012, March 14). Retrieved June 26, 2015, from http://runnersconnect.net/running-training-articles/how-much-does-age-effect-running-performance/

Hyperemesis Gravidarum: Signs, Symptoms and Treatment. (2012, April 26). Retrieved July 12, 2015, from http://americanpregnancy.org/pregnancy-complications/hyperemesis-gravidarum/

Kardel, K. (2005). Effects of intense training during and after pregnancy in top-level athletes. *Scand J Med Sci Sports Scandinavian Journal of Medicine and Science in Sports, 15*(2), 79-86.

Karp, J. (2013, April 10). Women's Hormones and Running - Guest Post by Jason Karp, Ph.D. Retrieved June 14, 2015, from http://ubermotherrunner.com/2013/04/10/womens-hormones-and-running-guest-post-by-jason-karp-ph-d/

Largest Races | Running USA. (2014). Retrieved April 10, 2015, from http://www.runningusa.org/largest-races

Lundgren, C. (2003). *Runner's world guide to running & pregnancy: How to stay fit, keep safe, and have a healthy baby.* Emmaus, Pennsylvania: Rodale Publishing Inc.

Muscle Tone. (n.d.). Retrieved July 26, 2015, from http://www.shapesense.com/fitness-exercise/articles/muscle-tone.aspx

Negishi, S., Li, Y., Usas, A., Fu, F., & Huard, J. (2005). The Effect of Relaxin Treatment on Skeletal Muscle Injuries. *The American Journal of Sports Medicine, 33*(12), 1816-1824. doi:10.1177/0363546505278701

Nielsen, R., Buist, I., Parner, E., Nohr, E., Sorensen, H., Lind, M., & Rasmussen, S. (2013). Predictors of Running-Related Injuries Among 930 Novice Runners: A 1-Year Prospective Follow-up Study. *Orthopaedic Journal of Sports Medicine, 1*(1). doi:10.1177/2325967113487316

O'Mara, K. (2013, October 3). Can Women Come Back Faster After Pregnancy? - Competitor.com. Retrieved June 1, 2015, from http://running.competitor.com/2013/10/training/can-women-come-back-faster-after-pregnancy_61244

Postpartum Depression. (n.d.). Retrieved June 3, 2015, from http://www.apa.org/pi/women/programs/depression/postpartum.aspx

Pregnant runner finishes 800 meters at U.S. nationals. (2014, June 27). Retrieved June 15, 2015, from http://www.usatoday.com/story/sports/olympics/2014/06/27/alysia-montano-34-weeks-pregnant-us-track-field-championships/11447031/

Pregnancy Nutrition - American Pregnancy Association. (2012, April 26). Retrieved June 5, 2015, from http://americanpregnancy.org/pregnancy-health/pregnancy-nutrition/

Prolactin Levels & Prolactin Testing. (2014). Retrieved June 7, 2015, from https://www.fertilityauthority.com/tests-and-medications/blood-tests-infertility/prolactin-levels

Prolactin: Sex and Immune Activation | Life Enhancement News. (2004, July 1). Retrieved August 2, 2015, from http://www.life-enhancement.com/magazine/article/966-prolactin-sex-and-immune-activation

Push Ups, Pull Ups & Pregnancy. (2015). Retrieved June 14, 2015, from http://www.askdoctornat.com/2013/01/07/exercise-intensity-in-pregnancy-hr-vs-rpe/

Quinn, T., Manley, M., Aziz, J., Padham, J., & Mackenzie, A. (2011). Aging and Factors Related to Running Economy. *Journal of Strength and Conditioning Research, 25*(11), 2971-2979. doi:10.1519/JSC.0b013e318212dd0e

Salvesen, K., Hem, E., & Sundgot-Borgen, J. (2011). Fetal wellbeing may be compromised during strenuous exercise among pregnant elite athletes. *British Journal of Sports Medicine, 46*(1), 279-283. doi:10.1136

Shutello, A. (2009, August 17). Women Athletes and Post Partum/Past Baby Knee Injuries. Retrieved July 14, 2015, from https://tighthams.wordpress.com/2009/08/18/women-athletes-and-post-partumpast-baby-knee-injuries/

Stangl, K., & Dschietzig, T. (2003). Relaxin: A pregnancy hormone as central player of body fluid and circulation homeostasis. *Cellular and Molecular Life Sciences (CMLS), 60*(4), 688-700.

Wallace, J., Ernsthausen, K., & Inbar, G. (1992). The Influence of the Fullness of Milk in the Breasts on the Concentration of Lactic Acid in Postexercise Breast Milk. *International Journal of Sports Medicine Int J Sports Med, 16*(2), 395-398.

Wallace, J., & Rabin, J. (1991). The Concentration of Lactic Acid in Breast Milk Following Maximal Exercise. *International Journal of Sports Medicine Int J Sports Med, 12*(3), 328-331.

Wolpert, K. (2009, October 6). A Runner's Guide to Jogging Strollers. Retrieved July 20, 2015, from http://www.runnersworld.com/rt-web-exclusive/a-runners-guide-to-jogging-strollers

Women's Health Care Physicians. (2002). Retrieved August 3, 2015, from http://www.acog.org/Resources_And_Publications/Committee_Opinions/Committee_on_Obstetric_Practice/Exercise_During_Pregnancy_and_the_Postpartum_Period?IsMobileSet=false

You & Your Hormones. (2010). Retrieved July 15, 2015, from http://www.yourhormones.info/hormones/relaxin.aspx

Yu, B., Kirkendall, D., & Garrett, W. (2002). Anterior Cruciate Ligament Injuries in Female Athletes: Anatomy, Physiology, and Motor Control.*Sports Medicine and Arthroscopy Review, 10*(1), 58-68. Retrieved June 10, 2015

Image Credits

All drawn images by Meredith Mikell.

All demonstration photography by Stephen Mikell Sr. & Stephen Mikell Jr.

Mighty Mama Photo credits:

Deena Kastor: credited to Deena Kastor

Michelle Baxter: credited to Michelle Baxter, www.therunnersplate.com

Lisa Valentine: credited to Chris Lauber, Florida Road Races, www.floridaroadraces.com

Christa Benton Stephens: credited to Christa Stephens

Stephanie Rothstein Bruce: credited to Stephanie Rothstein Bruce

Susan Empey: credited to Susan Empey

Pila Cadena: credited to Pila Cadena

Susan Iverson Casaway: credited to Susan Iverson Casaway

Nancy Smith: credited to Nancy Smith

Dr. Matt Maggio: credited to Peak Performance Sports Therapy LLC, www.peakperformancefl.com

About the Author

Meredith Mikell is a running mom and science teacher in St Petersburg, Florida. She grew up primarily in Washington state but graduated high school in central Arizona after successfully competing in both track and cross country. She attended Eckerd College to study marine biology and was also a member of the school's maritime search and rescue team. Meredith went on to teach science following graduation and completed her masters in aeronautical science two years later. It was while teaching high school science that she coached track and cross country, further motivating her to take her own running more seriously. She attributes successes in her own training to consistency, discipline, and a thirst to learn as much as possible about running physiology and new developments in training methodologies. Meredith currently runs for the Oiselle Volée Team and Nuun Hydration. Outside of teaching and running, Meredith focuses her time on her toddler son, Jack, her teenage stepson, Stephen Jr, and her husband and fellow teacher, Stephen Mikell Sr.

Check out Meredith's blog, *Runnervation: one runner's quest to reach her genetic potential*:

www.runnervation.com

Printed in Great Britain
by Amazon